Carleton Renaissance Plays in Translation

General Editors: Donald Beecher, Massimo Ciavolella

Editorial Advisors:

J. Douglas Campbell (Carleton)
Peter Clive (Carleton)
Louise George Clubb (Harvard)
Bruno Damiani (Catholic University of America)
Louise Fothergill-Payne (Calgary)
Peter Fothergill-Payne (Calgary)
Amilcare A. Iannucci (Toronto)
Jean-Marie Maguin (Montpellier)
Domenico Pietropaolo (Toronto)
Anthony Raspa (Chicoutimi)
José Ruano de la Haza (Ottawa)
Pamela Stewart (McGill)

Carleton Renaissance Plays in Translation offers the student, scholar, and general reader a selection of sixteenth-century masterpieces in modern English translation, most of them for the first time. The texts have been chosen for their intrinsic merits and for their importance in the history of the development of the theatre. Each volume contains a critical and interpretive introduction intended to increase the enjoyment and understanding of the text. Reading notes illuminate particular references, allusions, and topical details. The comedies chosen as the first texts have fast-moving plots filled with intrigues. The characters, though cast in the stock patterns of the genre, are witty and amusing portraits reflecting Renaissance social customs and pretensions. Not only are these plays among the most celebrated of their own epoch, but they directly influenced the development of the comic opera and theatre throughout Europe in subsequent centuries.

In print:

Odet de Turnèbe, *Satisfaction All Around (Les Contens)*
Translated with an Introduction and Notes by Donald Beecher

Annibal Caro, *The Scruffy Scoundrels (Gli Straccioni)*
Translated with an Introduction and Notes by Massimo Ciavolella
and Donald Beecher

Giovan Maria Cecchi, *The Owl (L'Assiuolo)*
Translated with an Introduction and Notes by Konrad Eisenbichler

Jean de La Taille, *The Rivals (Les Corrivaus)*
Translated with an Introduction and Notes by H.P. Clive

Alessandro Piccolomini, *Alessandro (L'Alessandro)*
Translated with an Introduction and Notes by Rita Belladonna

Gian Lorenzo Bernini, *The Impresario (Untitled)*
Translated with an Introduction and Notes by Donald Beecher and
Massimo Ciavolella

Jacques Grévin, *Taken by Surprise (Les Esbahis)*
Translated with an Introduction and Notes by Leanore Lieblein and
Russell McGillivray

Lope de Vega, *The Duchess of Amalfi's Steward (El mayordomo de la
duquesa de Amalfi)*
Translated with an Introduction and Notes by Cynthia Rodriguez-Badendyck

Comparative Critical Approaches to Rennaisance Comedy
Edited by Donald Beecher and Massimo Ciavolella

Pietro Aretino, *The Marescalco (Il Marescalco)*
Translated with an Introduction and Notes by Leonard G. Sbrocchi and
J. Douglas Campbell

Lope de Rueda, *The Interludes*
Translated with an Introduction and Notes by Randall W. Listerman

Girolamo Bargagli, *The Female Pilgrim (La Pellegrina)*
Translated with an Introduction and Notes by Bruno Ferraro

Leone de Sommi, *A Comedy of Betrothal (Tsahoth B'dihutha D'kiddushin)*
Translated with an Introduction and Notes by Alfred S. Golding in
consultation with Reuben Ahroni

*About the Harrowing of Hell: A Seventeenth-Century Ukrainian Play
in Its European Context*
Translated with an Introduction and Notes by Irena R. Makaryk

Hans Sachs, *Nine Carnival Plays*
Translated with an Introduction and Notes by Randall W. Listerman

Carleton Renaissance Plays in Translation

Hans Sachs

Nine Carnival Plays

Translated with an Introduction and Notes by

Randall W. Listerman

Dovehouse Editions Canada
1990

Canadian Cataloguing in Publication Data

Sachs, Hans, 1494–1576
    Nine carnival plays

(Carleton Renaissance plays in translation; 18)
Translated from the German.
Includes bibliographical references.

ISBN 0–919473–68–7

    I. Listerman, Randall W. (Randall Wayne), 1938–
II. Title. III. Series.

PT1763.A4 1990   832'.4   C90–090017–2

For distribution write to:
    Dovehouse Editions Inc.
    32 Glen Avenue
    Ottawa, Canada
    K1S 2Z7

For information on the series write to:
    Carleton Renaissance Plays in Translation
    Department of English
    Carleton University
    Ottawa, Canada
    K1S 5B6

Typeset by Humanities Publishing Services, University of Toronto.

Printed in Canada

Table of Contents

Acknowledgements 7

Introduction 9

    Notes to the Introduction 26

    Bibliography 29

Nine Carnival Plays

The Nose Dance 33

The Stolen Bacon 40

The Calf-Hatching 47

The Wife in the Well 54

The Farmer with the Blur 60

The Evil Woman 65

The Grand Inquisitor in the Soup 74

The Dead Man 82

The Pregnant Farmer 88

    Notes to the Texts 95

In memory of Miami University German Professors Charles Bangert and Jacques Breitenbucher. Their love of laughter still lives in the hearts of their former students and colleagues.

Acknowledgments

I owe an initial debt of gratitude to my former colleague Charles W. Bangert (1907–1978), who proposed the idea of this translation to me over a decade ago. I wish to thank Professors Carels and Miller for their scholarly advice and suggestions. I wish also to thank the General Editors, Professors Donald Beecher and Massimo Ciavolella, for their encouragement, immediate attention, and wise suggestions.

I wish to acknowledge the gracious support provided by Miami University: in particular I wish to thank Leonard J. Simutis, Dean of the Graduate School, for his gracious assistance; Dean Karl R. Mattox of the College of Arts and Science; and the Department of Spanish and Portuguese for aid drawn from the Faculty Fund. I would like to thank Betty Marak who typed the manuscript and frequently made order out of disorder.

My wife Layne and son Devin have not only foregone numerous family activities to the demands of my work schedule, but have also provided the encouragement which was needed to complete this edition.

Introduction

1. Historical Background of the Carnival Play

The *Fastnachtsspiel* was the earliest form of German secular drama, and as a dramatic form traces its origins to the pre-Lenten carnival of the late Middle Ages. Although the high point of this carnival theater was reached in the fifteenth and sixteenth centuries, the cultural roots of carnival itself extend far back into the spring rites of pre-Christian Europe. Among heathen nations it was customary to celebrate the victory of spring over winter at the time of the vernal equinox as a triumph of light and fertility over the waning period of darkness and barrenness. It was a time of celebration with rites and dancing that incorporated into the traditions of the festival vestiges of that cosmic struggle in the form of ludic contests.

The battle between winter and spring was a favorite theme of medieval German epics and ballads and frequently took the form of a dramatic dialogue. Other pagan themes received similar treatment in dialogic poetry and doggerel, including the sordid and ribald ballads peddled by "jugglers" and street singers. Public presentation of such repertory items, initially limited to court festivals, gradually invaded the marketplace. The village square or marketplace provided an ideal location for non-dramatic entertainment (story-telling, singing, dancing, tumbling, and juggling) as well as for dramatic presentations. The biggest presentation day was Shrove Tuesday, the last day of carnival time.[1] For this occasion the butcher-mummers (*Schembartläufer*) put on their pagan cultic pageantry and dances. And for this occasion also other burghers — partly to compete with the butcher-mummer guilds — put on more moral presentations. In this way, the first peculiarly German drama was developed: the *Fastnachtsspiel*, the carnival or Shrovetide play.

Scholars have several theories about the origin of the word "Fastnacht." In combination with *fasten*, "to fast," *Fastnacht* means the time before the fast. Because of the worldly nature of *Fastnacht*, some consider the root word to be the middle High German verb *vaseln*,

meaning "to thrive or be fertile."[2] Wilhelm Wackernagel believed that
the first component of the word was not taken from *fasten* (to fast)
but rather from *fasen* or *faseln* (to talk nonsense, to have fun). He
submitted that *Fastnacht* would thus denote an evening of feasting
and fooling.[3] He also stated that the popular interpretation in medieval
times could easily have meant a time of carousing and application to
the *Fass* (cask). Whatever the accuracy of these various etymologi-
cal interpretations, they are certainly applicable to the spirit of Hans
Sachs's *Fastnachtsspiele*.

The first allusion to the *Fastnachtsspiel* was in 1426 in Hall, Tirol.
References to *Fastnachtsspiele* in other localities can be found in many
city chronicles throughout Germany.[4] The genre existed until the beginning of the seventeenth century, but waned as learned, scholarly
writers began to disdain its vulgar origins. The city of Nuremberg is
where its development can best be seen. It is in this old Bavarian city
where Hans Sachs lived, wrote, and performed in his carnival plays.

During *Fastnacht*, the shoemakers (like Sachs), the carpenters,
smiths, butchers, bakers, and all the tradesmen gathered together and
indulged in drinking, dancing and the telling of riddles, jokes and ribald stories for the entertainment of all present. It was a time to be
completely free from social restrictions and was dedicated solely to
gratification and amusement. It may be that competition between the
guilds led to combats of wits among members and bids in their story-
telling to provoke the most laughter. In any event, the oldest of this type
of *Fastnachtsspiel*, or the sequential play (*Rheihenspiel*), consisted of
several characters delivering a series of humorous monologues. Gradually a general framework for the carnival play developed. One person
became a spokesperson for the group, introducing other participating
members of the play to the audience. This later development or evo-
lution of the *spiel* (play) came to be known as the *Handlungspiel*, or
simply, "plot play." Instead of someone narrating a joke or explaining
what two or more persons said, the parts were acted out. At the con-
clusion of the play, the spokesperson frequently invited the audience
to join in a dance with the actors or to buy drinks for the group. Often
there was interaction between the performers and the audience.

Unlike modern drama, which attempts to create a reality of its own,
the *Fastnachtsspiel* in the time of Hans Sachs was an integral part of
the revelry. Rather than disengage the audience from its bacchanalian
festivity, the play tended to bring the public into the dramatic activity.
This characteristic is easily recognizable in any of the many Hans Sachs

plays. An actor may address the audience directly, pay them false compliments, and invite them to celebrate themselves with a drink, as in the opening lines of *The Evil Woman*. The mayor, in the first play of this edition, *The Nose-Dance*, exhorts and invites the spectators to step forward and join the communal dance. Who has the biggest nose to win the prize and lead the dance? Everybody — farmers, burghers, rich and poor, men and women, boys and girls — is invited to join the parade and participate in the fun and frolic.

The plays of carnival, then, were performed by members of the community as they strolled about town in the course of the celebration; they began and ended within the context of carnival. Groups of revelers established themselves at a convenient tavern,[5] house, or other public place. The humorous and simple content of the plays as well as their short length (an average of 350 lines) facilitated their performance and production.

The *Fastnachtsspiele* dealt with everyday situations, including family scenes, peasant settings, and the immorality of the priests. The material of the plays themselves was simple, traditional, and easily understood. The favorite characters were familiar individuals, such as the farmer, whose stupidity and gullibility were legendary among the city dwellers. The dominant theme was the exposure of human folly, especially the follies of the farmer or peasant by the moral burghers. Unfortunately, the popularity of comedy and carnival farce did not continue to evolve and develop in Germany at this time. The exigencies of the Reformation and the devastating effects of the thirty years of relentless civil war stalemated the German theater at the very moment when it was beginning the same ascent as the theater in England, Spain, and France. Sachs died in 1576, and almost two centuries were to elapse before Germany could again make a valid contribution to the drama.

The center for the development of the *Fastnachtsspiel* was Nuremberg, and there are four known authors who lived and wrote there. The first, Hans Rosenplüt, to whom a dozen such plays are ascribed, wrote in the middle of the fifteenth century. His plays give bold Nurembergian moral and political advice, but have achieved little lasting fame or literary distinction. Hans Folz (1450–1515), born in Worms, settled in Nuremberg and wrote at least eight *Fastnachtsspiele*. *König Solomon und Markolf* (*King Solomon and Markolf*) and *Ein hübsch Vastnachtspil* (*A Nice Carnival Play*) were among his best and reflect the development of the genre. The acknowledged master of the *Fastnachtsspiel* was Hans Sachs, who, as he put it, "was a shoemaker and poet too." Sachs is more fully discussed later in this introduction.

The fourth Nuremberger, Jakob Ayrer (1540–1605), continued the tradition of the *Fastnachtsspiel*. Like Hans Sachs, he also wrote tragedies and comedies that had little enduring success. Altogether, he wrote sixty-nine plays of which thirty-six are grouped together as carnival plays. A transitional figure, Ayrer moved toward farce, copying some of the ribaldry of the Elizabethan drama (then beginning to reach Germany) and introducing the figure of the jester in its popular, clownish form with the name Hans Wurst ("Hans Sausage"). Performed little, Ayrer's plays received more attention when they were published posthumously in 1618. Jakob Ayrer is remembered chiefly as a transitional figure in the trend from the popular *Fastnachtsspiel* of the Renaissance to the Baroque classical drama of the seventeenth century.

The characters or actors in the carnival plays and farces all shared a similar spirit and are motivated by the same attitude of playing, celebrating and reveling. Their very essence was to create an ethos reflective of and compatible with carnival celebration. This essence explains their interest in food, wine, sex, and their sheer love of waggery. What Donald Beecher has convincingly argued in his study on intriguers and tricksters is characteristic of all the *Fastnachtsspiele personae*. The trickster is, "to a very large extent, the archetypal embodiment of the impulse for play, and it is this 'attitude' that preserves the integrity of the type. . . . The trickster delights in creating confusion and mayhem when it serves his ends. . . . He is ready to suspend mores and public decency in order to turn society on its head, whether for fun or profit. The urge to win, dominate, compromise or expose by deception and the pre-calculated ploy, and to do it with ingenuity and panache is his defining complexion."[6] The trickster archetype that Beecher describes is especially appropriate to the characters of Hans Sachs.

The trickster is one of Sachs's favorite dramatic characters. For example, in two of the carnival plays included in this edition, Sachs features a female intriguer. In the play entitled *The Wife in the Well*, Gitta, the wife, not only dupes her unsuspecting husband but successfully implicates him as the guilty party.

STEFFANO: Woe is me. Am I the most miserable of men? I'm out womanned by a crafty wife, both in body and soul. I've suspected her for a long time, but she sure can out-trick me. I even end up being the guilty one. Pushed and slapped on top of that.

In the other play, entitled *The Farmer with the Blur*, Gretta represents the height of successful roguery. Gretta's skill and art not only
save her neighbor Christa from an assured physical beating, but win
Christa a new red purse as well.

CHRISTA: Oh my husband has such heavy hands. Believe me, I've
felt them before. I know how he gets even. I don't trust him.
GRETTA: Dear neighbor, just stay home and bake your husband a cake.
I'll go out in the forest and talk to your husband. I'll think of some
trick to play on him. He's as dumb as the Almighty's horse. I
take that back. He's more ass than horse. I'll use my cunning
wits to calm him down and make him forget his anger.

It has been said that "the bare unaccommodated trickster is on
perennial holiday from conformity."[7] It is this same perennial holiday
of nonconformity that gives carnival time its spirit and attitude. Carnival provided Hans Sachs a large degree of insulation from reprisal
from the individuals and institutions that he satirized in his plays. The
attitude and reality of pre-Lent afforded Sachs the freedom to portray
and poke fun at those characters who symbolized corruption, naiveté,
pride, venality, lasciviousness, greed, and other follies and foibles of his
countrymen.

Carnival marked the suspension of all hierarchical rank, privileges,
norms, and prohibitions. Carnival was the true feast of time, the feast of
becoming, change, and renewal. Everybody was equal during carnival.
There, in the town square, a special form of free and familiar contact
reigned among people who were usually divided by the barriers of caste,
property, profession, and age.[8] Mikhail Bakhtin has correctly suggested,
I believe, that carnival laughter was the laughter of all the people—
universal in scope—directed at all and everyone, including the carnival
participants themselves. The entire world was seen in its gay relativity.
The laughter of carnival was ambivalent, hilarious, triumphant, and at
the same time mocking and deriding. It asserted and denied, buried and
revived. In fact, carnival throughout all of Europe and parts of Latin
America has probably changed very little over the centuries; ribaldry,
rascality, and merry-making still reign supreme and in varying degrees
before the repentance and contrition of Ash Wednesday once again
balances the collective social scale.

In a recent study on the subject entitled *Carnival and Theater*,
Michael Bristol describes perceptively that carnival provided, to a great
extent, the *mise en scène* or backdrop for a great deal of European

drama. Carnival time, he asserts, "provided plebian culture with an alternative world in which the closed ranks and status groups of the social structure ceased being the rational norm. An alternative view of social reality was enacted by a group of Carnival personae who reveled and revealed by their mimicry that rule and misrule can be of equivocal and of unstable nature."[9]

Such was the milieu that embraced, embodied, and to a real degree emboldened the most significant dramatic works of Hans Sachs — the carnival plays. It was an environment in which the Nuremberg playwright dramatized and satirized his contemporaries with the larger context of the carnival celebration itself. His plays are like dramatic microcosms existing with their own identies within the carnivalesque cosmos of sixteenth-century Germany. This quality is seen clearly in the first play of this edition, *The Nose-Dance.*

MAYOR: Alright everybody. Your attention please! Over here. Turn around! I have an announcement. All you farmers know good ol' cousin Gunker from Rebenstein. Why he owns most of the town. Well, he was nice enough to send us these three prizes you see hangin' here on this stick. Yep, it's all for our Nose-Dance celebration.

. . . .

So that everybody gets a chance to prove his point, let each and all pass before me. Don't be shy. Step right up single file so I can judge each nose with the measuring cup and ruler.

This particular carnival play, as the majority of the others, is invitational. It exhorts anyone and everyone to participate. Carnival plays were not equipped with footlights, in the sense that they did not acknowledge any distinction between actors and spectators. Footlights would have destroyed a carnival play in Sachs's day, just as the absence of footlights would probably destroy a theatrical performance today. Carnival was not a spectacle seen by the people; they lived it and frequently acted in it themselves. All the people were invited to participate in varying degrees, to physically "dance" and not be shy.

It has been suggested that as long as carnival lasted, there was no life outside it. Life and life's activities were subject to the laws of carnival time — laws emanating from its own freedom and universal spirit. A special condition pervaded the entire world which called for the world's revival and the renewal of all.[10] One feels a sense of this special condition upon reading a *Fastnachtsspiel.* There is an ebullient perception of life renewing and rewinding itself. There is a sensation of continuum. The carnival plays do not end in the classic or generic way that other comedies do with a typical "all's well that ends well" closure. The structural tempo of these plays suggests on-going activity. The plot or story at the end appears to be suspended only for the moment. The last lines of many carnival plays are open-ended, inviting the conception of yet another play in cyclical, unending fashion. In this edition's *The Stolen Bacon* the tempo is clearly protracted.

PRIEST: So come on, let's roll out a good wine and be happy with each other. Let's go over to the rectory courtyard and drink 'til daybreak. Let Hermann go gnaw on bones because he can't enjoy goodness. He buries and ruins it. . . . So that the tightwad's money sack doesn't get too big—that's what wishes Hans Sachs.

Kunz, in the play, *The Pregnant Farmer*, also makes indelibly clear that the play's time-frame will be prolonged to enhance his carnival time.

KUNZ: . . . When six weeks are up, I'll just take it easy for a while around the kitchen like the old and real young do. We'll go spend our carnival time with others. Let fun, frolic and good times chase away sadness and misfortune. This is what Hans Sachs and his actors wish for you.

A spirit of prolonged *carpe diem* is the essence of the Sachsian comedies. Created in a spirit of renewal and rejuvenation, his plays are like children of carnival itself in that they are ever-changing, playful, appropriately irreverent, and exude excitement for "turnabout" and "make-believe." Parody, travesty, humiliation, profanation of comic crownings and uncrownings are the hallmarks of his festive drama.

2. Hans Sachs, Life

There is something to be said for the age as well as the man who, as a cobbler, could become a humanist, a poet, a musician, acquire a good library, learn Greek literature and philosophy, write 6,000 poems and live in reasonable health and happiness until he was eighty-two.

Hans Sachs was born six years before the end of the fifteenth century and lived until 1576. Hans, the son of a tailor, at the age of seven began his schooling at the *Nuremberg Spitalschule*. His teacher, one Herr Friedel, taught him grammar, geography, singing, and later on some Latin. For eight years he remained in this school, but that was the only formal schooling he ever received.[11]

At the age of seventeen, in 1511, Hans Sachs embarked on his *wanderjahre*. From Regensburg, where he first stopped and remained for two months, he went on to Passau, and from there down the Inn River, via Braunau, Ried, and Wells to Salzburg. Everywhere he interested himself not only in his training as a cobbler, but also in the life of the many people with whom he came into contact. Rudolph Genée has suggested that "his youthful, pleasing appearance as well as his open personality and his sense of ambition won for him everywhere friendship and advocacy."[12]

During these formative years, Sachs's interest in literature, as well as in people, grew rapidly. His earliest dated and preserved literary attempt was written in 1513. This was a *Buhlscheidlied* in which he describes the pangs of separation from a beloved. About this same time, it is equally significant to note that he obtained a copy of the Augsburg edition of Heinrich Steinhöwels' translation (approximately 1480) of Boccaccio's *Decameron*.[13] In 1514 Sachs continued his travels to Munich, then to Würzburg, Frankfurt am Main, Koblenz, and Cologne. He returned to his native Nuremberg in 1516.

On September 1, 1519 he was married to Kunigunde Kreuzer. This union lasted until her death forty-one years later. All seven of his children died before his wife died. Seventeen months after the death of Kunigunde, he took a second wife, a young girl by the name of Barbara Harscher. Despite his advanced years (sixty-eight) and the wide disparity in their ages (Barbara was twenty-seven), this marriage, too, seems to have been happy. His life during these years was apparently the life of a typically industrious and successful artisan of his day.

The literary production of Sachs is enormous. For example, in his *Summa all meiner Gedichte von 1514 Jar an bis 1567 Jar*, Sachs himself lists 4,275 works. Adalbert Keller, his principal bibliographer, corroborates this fact.[14] Hans Sachs wrote *Erzählungen* (tales), *Schwänke* (farces), *Fabeln* (fables), and a vast number of *Lieder* (songs, poems). For a time, his relationship with the Lutheran reformation was an active participation. In 1523 he published his famous defense of Martin Luther, the *Wittembergisch Nachtigall* (*Wittemberger Nightingale*), and four years later appeared a group of Reformation prose dialogues. His dramatic works include: sixty-one tragedies, sixty-five comedies, and eighty-five *Fastnachtsspiele* of which nine are translated in this edition.

The consensus of critics of German literature seems to be that: "great as were his achievements in all phases of German literature, Hans

Sachs's art is at its best in the *Fastnachtsspiele.*"[15] Johann Wolfgang von Goethe, in a poem much in the style of Hans Sachs, honored the poet with:

> A wreath of oak with leaves eternally green
> Placed on his brow by those succeeding him.
> And to the frogpond banished be
> All those who failed to pay their master heed![16]

Goethe freely admitted to the influence of Sachs's carnival plays in the following way: "they capture life, mankind in all his wonderful texture, the confusion, chaos, searching, jostling, pushing, pressing and rubbing (of human activity)."[17]

In addition to Sachs's commitment to his creative works, he was also involved in the issues of his day. For example, in 1521, the works of Martin Luther came into his hands.[18] He made a thorough study of the Reformation movement and finally committed himself to its cause. In 1523 he published *Die Wittembergisch Nachtigall* (*The Wittemberg Nightingale*), a song of praise that defended Martin Luther as well as established his reputation as a writer.

Such a poem, written by a shoemaker, had to create an impression, and it quickly spread among the people in all of Germany. The malpractices perpetrated on the Christian faith by the clergy were herein described with authority and in such vivid language that we still marvel at it today. . . .[19]

His religious conviction brought him fame and, as expected, some criticism. But no critic could discourage him. Hans Sachs poured out his mastersongs, poems and other works in amounts which must astonish us. As a *Meistersinger*, Sachs and many of his contemporaries were members of German guilds of poets and singers who attempted to preserve the medieval art form of the *Minnesingers* (songs of love). The *Meistersingers*, of whom the most famous were Hans Sachs and Hans Folz, usually formed organizations similar to the craft guilds of their day. The title of "master" was given only to those who had proven their creative and vocal talent in singing contests between the poets and singers of other guilds. In this historical context, Richard Wagner immortalized Hans Sachs as the kindly guiding genius in his comic opera *Die Meistersinger von Nürnberg* in 1868.

As one might expect, Hans Sachs's earnings had to come almost exclusively from his trade rather than from his writings, and yet he managed to live quite comfortably. There are, however, vague references to be found stressing that in later volumes of his songs and poems he no longer called himself "shoemaker."[20] Still, he must have somehow found time for both his trade and his artistic endeavors. A case in point is on record from 1527. In that year Sachs, working with the preacher of *Lorenzkirche*, Andreas Osiander, published *Die Weisung von Papsttum* (*The Directive from the Papacy*). It appears that Osiander had found some documents with illustrations in a Carthusian monastery in Nuremberg. They had been written in the thirteenth century and seemed to predict the downfall of the papacy. Osiander asked Sachs to set rhymes to some of the illustrations. Although the city council had decided for Protestantism in 1525, and had even closed some of the monasteries and ordered the removal of concubines, it considered the pamphlet to be dangerous. The council confiscated and destroyed all of the pamphlets it could find. Osiander, Sachs, and the publisher received severe reprimands from the council.[21]

It is equally well documented that Sachs was an avid reader, and that he had an impressive library for a man of his time.[22] This library furnished him with hours of pleasant reading and sources for his works. By 1517, Sachs had written his first *Fastnachtsspiel*. Before 1549 he had only written sixteen of them, but between 1549 and 1554 he had written thirty-five more. By the time he completed his last *Fastnachtsspiel* in 1560, he had composed, by his account, eighty-five. The tragedies and comedies, mentioned previously, he wrote and acted in as the theatrical director in Nuremberg. These dramatic works were first presented in *St. Marta Kirch* and the *Dominikanerkloster*. As the material became more worldly, the dramas were presented in the larger inns and in the courtyards in front of the inns.

Comedies, tragedies, and carnival plays and poems all poured from the restless pen of Sachs, to "God's praise, fame and glory," as he says in his autobiographical poem "Valete." His first wife had now died, he had remarried, and he was living to a ripe old age. His years, however, did not leave him untouched. He gives the reason for calling his poem "Valete":

> For old age does much to vex me,
> to press, weigh down, and confine me.[23]

Undoubtedly, his last years were enhanced by the presence of his quite young and apparently attractive Barbara, whose beauty and winning ways he could not find words enough to praise. Perhaps it was she, while the old *Meister's* senses became duller — his hearing and his sight began to fail — who was responsible for the fact that the quiet good humor so evident in his writings never deserted him. He died on the

19th of January 1576, and was buried in the "Johannisfriedhof" in Nuremberg. His gravesite is unknown.

Life in Nuremberg continued as before, but perhaps ever so slightly changed, wanting the nimble mind and restless pen of Hans Sachs, poet, cobbler, and honored patriarch who rests somewhere within its walls.

3. The Production of the Plays

An impressive number of theater groups actually existed and operated in Nuremberg at the time of Hans Sachs. Many groups, guilds, and visiting troupes of the *commedia dell'arte*,[24] usually led by one author-actor-producer, competed for the places the city made available for the performance of plays. Hans Sachs, in addition to performing and staging his plays in public houses and taverns, produced his plays in a host of different places. For example, they were performed at the "preacher's cloister," the "Clarakirche," the "Lorenzkirche," city hall, the "Frauenbrüderkloster," the "Hallsbrunnerhof," the "Augustinerkloster," the "Spital," and the "Golden Swan."[25] The minutes of the Nuremberg city council furnish a record of applications for the use of these facilities by various groups, as well as the council's decisions in such matters. Petitions were by no means evaluated on the basis of available space only.

The city fathers would grant no such permission without first having acquainted themselves with the play in question and approving the script. The inspection of such scripts was not simply perfunctory, and censorship occurred. For example, on January 15, 1551, we find that Hans Sachs's play *About the Abbot and a Nobleman* was declined "with good words" because its performance might prove detrimental.[26] The play, entitled *Das Wildbad*, was a *Fastnachtsspiel* written in 1550. The city council obviously did not wish to offend the nobles residing outside the city who made their living by means similar to those of the robber-baron in the play.

Once the necessary approval from the city fathers was obtained and permission was granted for a performance in a hall, square, or church courtyard, the place had to be equipped with a stage. There is disagreement as to the details of the stage and exact location within the hall or church grounds, but it is generally accepted that the stage consisted of a platform with steps leading up to it and facilities for entrances and exits.

There was no semblance of a complete set or set-design at the time. A certain amount of standard props were used such as towers, bushes, house facades, and trees. The sets were used to suggest, not to represent, the locality where the scene was to take place. They had to be moved, which of necessity was done in full view of the audience.

There is some similarity to the Elizabethan theater in England, but the theater of Hans Sachs was far less sophisticated. There is only one platform, no curtained sections, no balconies. But the audience must have accepted the limitations willingly and, when given a suggestion of the setting, supplied the rest from their own imaginations. Strange enough, however, there is reference to the audience's insistence on realism in small details deemed nonessential in earlier as well as later times. Köster refers to the anticipation of audiences to actually see weapons, letters, everything edible, "occasionally fire and smoke, beatings dealt out, and bloodshed"[27] realistically represented, while they were quite willing to take a single bush to signify a garden.

As in the Elizabethan theater, changes of scene are numerous and happen in rapid succession. Had there been more than fragmentary settings, if any, an unbearable amount of time would have been taken up in shifting scenery. As it was, all that had to happen to change a scene was the exit of all the characters. The next actor/character entering would establish the new locale. For example, in *The Calf-Hatching* we find the husband at home, complaining he overslept and let things get out of hand. At the end of his lines, Sachs merely indicates his exit, whereupon the wife enters on her way from the market. Her first line, "Whew! Well, I've been to town. Wonder how that vermin kept house while I was gone," sets the scene and establishes a new milieu. At times Hans Sachs hints at the upcoming locale to aid the audience's visualization. So in *The Pregnant Farmer*, Kunz the farmer prepares us for the next scene, the home of the Jew, with a short remark, "Heinz, take this glass of my urine and ride like crazy to Sentelbach. Go to the inn and ask for the Jewish doctor, Isaac." When moments later the stage is cleared and Isaac enters, we must assume that we are now at his inn. Isaac's opening lines do not indicate his whereabouts at all. Granted, this method had the subtlety of a hammer, but subtlety was not one of the strengths of Hans Sachs or his theater. Nevertheless, clearing the stage for a moment is still successfully employed today in plays with non-localized settings, a testimony to the method's effectiveness.

Musical interludes were not unknown at the time to bridge the transition from one scene to another or to cover for a fast shift of props, although Hans Sachs does not give directions to that effect in any of his plays. Costumes were simply the dress of the time, with an occasional "Turkish" costume tossed in to denote a foreign character. Props, such as crowns, weapons, or horrible masks for the devil, completed the dress of the actors.

As to the actors themselves, they were primarily tradesmen of Nuremberg. Rudolph Genée quotes from an unidentified manuscript:

The oldest actors, and still at the time of Hans Sachs, were all simple and common people, mostly meistersingers. But there are reports that some of them played these parts superbly. A certain Häublein was a master at pitiable parts and made all the spectators cry. Teisinger was a sober fellow and very adept at playing the Emperor of Turkey or even the Devil. Perschla, a young man and brushmaker, played a maiden so well that no woman could do better.[28]

The style of acting in the *Fastnachtsspiel* was simple and fittingly realistic for its purpose. Sachs's language, while in verse form, is simple and straight to the point, probably very close to the usage in sixteenth-century Nuremberg.

How might these plays be produced, directed, performed today? The first clue may be the sparseness of stage directions in Sachs's originals. While certain hints are given now and then, all details are left open for the creative spirit of actor and director to take over and expand. Several styles might be imposed upon the plays if a director so chooses. For example, a *commedia dell'arte* setting and style might enhance a production, giving it a different point of departure. It seems to me that the main factor in the production of any of the plays is the mood. Many characters, who upon first reading may appear dull and two-dimensional, can, with a little imagination and involvement, begin to sparkle and display qualities and facets one wouldn't expect to find. The performance should exude the exuberant feeling of a small-town fair, which had to be present at the performances in Nuremberg. Without such a feeling, "attitude," or mood, a contemporary performance would simply be a dusted relic complete with naive lines and flat-footed humor.

Any performance of these plays — whether professional or amateur — must provide enjoyment for an audience. If it does not solve their problems, it at least permits them a glimpse of a time when similar problems existed and formed part of human existence four hundred years ago.

4. Characters

The *Handlungspiel* ("plot play"), the consequent and logical development of the earlier *Rheihenspiel* ("recitation play"), constituted the
beginnings of the development of modern German drama and the transition to actual representation from mere recitation. It was in the *Handlungspiel* as it gradually evolved that one can see the beginnings of
individualizing characterization. Though Hans Rosenplüt and Hans
Folz had already achieved a certain degree of success with their dramatic characters, it was not until the *Fastnachtsspiele* of Hans Sachs
that characterization of individual figures really succeeded. Sachs con-
sciously amplified and individualized his characters in order to inject
into his plays a new dramatic reality. A theatrical expert, he real-
ized the impact of well-developed characters. He did not just re-create
types, but rather varied them significantly by means of enlargement
and enrichment. Hans Knudsen in his history of German theater has
written: "The typical characters in Hans Sachs serve to reveal theatri-
cally general human weakness, but in such a manner that their singular
characteristics allow them to appear as individually different."[29]

Quite often Sachs used peasant characters. (In fact, five of the nine
plays in our selection feature peasant characters.) The peasant, barely
liberated from serfdom, was looked down upon with open amusement
by the prosperous new class of burghers which Hans Sachs represents
and for whom, to a large extent , he wrote his plays. Sachs did little
to change the stereotypical conception of the peasant; if anything he
reinforced it. But the feet of clay he gives them are found in everyone.
Here citizens of Nuremberg could laugh while watching plays aimed at
their country cousins. But could they, at least the thinking ones among
them, completely escape the feeling that somehow they too were being
portrayed?

The peasant was Sachs's favorite representative of the comic ele-
ment. Vail Pig-Pen (Velle Mistfink), Herman Brainless (Herman Hirn-
los), Freddie Dungheap (Friedlein Zettenscheiss), Kunz Turnip-fumes
(Kuntz Rubendunst), the farmers' wives, all the peasants are certainly
comic figures. The peasant character in the plays is foolish, sly, not always honest, calculating, and frequently self-defeating in his schemes.
But he is also an individual, not completely a stereotype, with a certain
innate "savvy" which makes him a challenge to the performer and an
audience.

Sachs by no means confined his humorous persecution to the country folk. There was plenty of wit to spill over onto other groups such as the clergy. Sachs never neglected a chance to deal a blow to a clergyman. While he, as mentioned previously, was an ardent supporter of Martin Luther and the Reformation, his attacks generally were not pointed at Catholicism *per se*. He preferred to shoot his arrows at the man rather than the religious faith the individual represented. At that time, all priests were by no means always pillars of society and moral examples to their flock. The clergy stands accused of immorality and corruption in three plays in this edition: *The Stolen Bacon, The Grand Inquisitor in the Soup*, and *The Farmer with the Blur*. The priest, in his own way, becomes a comic figure as well under Sachs's treatment. He was used for amusement as much as didactic accusation. The reason for placing the priest in this position may be two-fold, stemming both from the behavior of the priests themselves and from the general joy of poking fun at a person in a superior position. To be sure, the three representations of the priesthood herein are not respectable or praiseworthy. Sachs shows little mercy with their shortcomings. Nevertheless, the treatment is one of indulgent criticism rather than a broadside of partisan condemnation and judgment.

Marital strife presents another rewarding point of attack for the Nuremberg farceur, as do the members of the female sex who usually cause it. But again, no matter whether it is aimed (by proxy, via country folk) at Nuremberg's fair sex in general or at married women or at old ones or evil ones, he seldom tries to injure. As one critic expresses it, "Hans Sachs classifies women — in jest — as an evil, a bother, which one has to contend with, since they are there anyhow. . . ."[30]

Needless to say the married woman is a special target. Indeed, all the women in this collection of *Fastnachtsspiele* are married. The young, unmarried woman, perhaps not fitting Sachs's moralizing purposes, is neglected in his plays. One can readily observe in this selection from *The Wife in The Well, The Farmer with the Blur, The Evil Woman*, and *The Dead Man*, that the women are nasty, sneaky, dominating, scheming, and calculating. They do their utmost to subjugate and control their men. But even in the coarsest fabric of their make-up we find snatches of love, woven there by a playwright who exaggerated faults, condemned them, but always found it possible, if not to excuse, at least to try to understand them.

Wives, husbands, and their struggles then supply much of the comic raw material for the carnival plays. From the earliest of comedies to the most modern, sophisticated, situational comedy of television today, marital strife has been exploited. Among the playwrights who have dealt with family squabbles throughout the ages, Hans Sachs is one of the most comical.

As a playwright, Hans Sachs shows crudeness in the construction of his carnival plays; the simplicity of language, while at times effective, sometimes works against him. But if he is seen against the background of theater as it existed at his time, in his part of the world, his significance and importance become clear. His greatness undoubtedly stems from his insight into human character, his fascination with human behavior, which, seldom changing, gives his simple playlets a timeless quality and charm. His plays were then, and are now, compelling pieces of theater, ideally suited for performance, full of the spirit of carnival and fun. They contain in their simplicity the spark of theatrical performance, and they can be successfully performed. It is my hope that these translations might offer encouragement and help to that end.

5. Notes on Translation

The primary purpose of this text is to present a modern, idiomatic translation of Hans Sachs's carnival plays. While I tried to give a close translation of the plays, I was always aware of the virtual impossibility of achieving a completely faithful rendering from a linguist's point of view. The task of translating Sachs's *knittelvers* or four-stress line rhymed in couplets (the verse form of all the carnival plays) into idiomatic English prose posed a substantial challenge. I regretted the loss of this poetic form, but after several adaptations in verse in the style of Hans Sachs, I came to see that while the results might amuse scholars, the general reader would find them alien and the actor impossible to recite with conviction.

I chose as texts for the basis of my translation the editions of Edmund Goetze, *Sämtliche Fastnachtsspiele von Hans Sachs in chronologischen Ordnung nach den Origenalen* (Halle, 1880) and the editions of the *Bibliothek des Litterarisch vereins* (Stuttgart, 1882) edited by A. V. Keller and E. Goetze. These sources among the earliest of the printed sources are generally accepted as faithful versions of Hans Sachs's works. These primary collections contain not only the carnival plays, comedies, and tragedies, but also a selection of his poems, songs, *schwänke* (farces), prose works, and a personal inventory of his library. Of the eighty-five listed carnival plays, I have selected nine which have not been translated into English. I have tried to select plays which show the development of Sachs as a playwright over the span of nearly a decade (1550–1559). In addition, I have attempted to select those plays which are the most dramatically invigorating, and hopefully, ones that might inspire successful presentation.

Some German editions of Sachs's carnival plays have been updated or *sprachlich erneuert*, and their editors have seemed to feel the necessity to modernize the playlets by transforming the earthy language of the originals into more cultivated and refined forms. The process, it seems to me, has resulted in labored and often awkward renditions. I have resisted this tendency and tried to translate faithfully Sachs's original language and forms of usage.

It is my hope that this edition will fulfill the need for a modern English translation of some of the carnival plays of Germany's foremost sixteenth-century playwright. The plays have lively theatrical qualities, and their stage production should not be confined exclusively to German-speaking countries. I am hopeful that these translations will serve to suggest how rich an asset they are to the living repertory of world theater.

NOTES TO THE INTRODUCTION

1 Eckehard Catholy, *Fastnachtsspiele* (Stuttgart: J. B. Metzlersche Verlags-buchhandlung, 1966), 10.

2 Friedrich Kluge, *Etymologisches Wörterbuch der deutschen Sprache*, 20th ed. revised by Walther Mitzka (Berlin: Walter de Gruyter & Co., 1967), 186.

3 Wilhelm Wackernagel, *Geschichte der deutschen Literatur* (Basle, 1848), 314.

4 Catholy, 6

5 There are many specific references to the tavern where the action is actually taking place. For example, one *Fastnachtsspiel* (53) says explicitly: "Ihr erbern Frauen und züchtige Herren, Ich komme zu euch in die *Taffern*, zu haben mit Euch ein guten Mut, wie man jetzt zu Fastnacht tut."

6 Donald A. Beecher, *Comparative Critical Approaches to Renaissance Comedy* (Ottawa, 1986), 67.

7 Beecher, 67.

8 Mikhail Bakhtin, *Rabelais and His World* (Cambridge, 1985), 27.

9 Michael Bristol, *Carnival and Theater* (New York, 1985), 27.

10 Bakhtin, 7.

11 Rudolph Genée, *Hans Sachs und seine Zeit* (Leipzig, 1894), 43. See also Barbara Könneker, *Hans Sachs*, (Stuttgart, 1971), 1.

12 Genée, 62. "Seine jugendfrisch und angenehme Erscheinung, dabei sein offenes Wesen und sein strebsamer Sinn erwarben ihm allenthalben bald Freundschaft und Fürsprachen."

13 Thirteen of Sachs's eighty-five listed carnival plays — four (29, 33, 48, and 55) were never published and have not been found — are either inspired by or are direct adaptations of the *Decameron*. See Randall W. Lister-man, "The Boccaccian Influence in the Dramatic Craftsmanship of Hans Sachs," *University of Dayton Review*, 10 (1983), 99–105.

14 Adalbert Keller, *Fastnachtsspiele* 11 (Stuttgart, 1858), 54.

15 Maximilian J. Rudwin, *The Origin of the German Carnival Comedy* (New York, 1920), 55. Rudwin further declares, "The Carnival comedy reached the zenith of its development in the hands of the Nuremberg cobbler-bard. Hans Sachs may indeed be called the father of the German secular drama."

16 From "Erklärung eines alten Holzschnittes, vorstellend Hans Sachsens poetische Sendung," first printed in "Teutsches Merkur," 1776, Aprilheft, 75.

  Ein Eichenkranz, ewig jung belaubt,
  Den setzt die Nachtwelt ihm aufs Haupt:
  In Froschpfuhl all das Volk verbannt,
  Das seinen Meister je verkannt!

17 Hélène Cattanés, *Les Fastnachtspiele de Hans Sachs* (Strasbourg, 1923),

16.
...alles Leben,
der Menschen wunderliches Weben,
Ihr Wirren, Suchen, Stossen und Treiben,
Schieben, Reissen, Drängen und Reiben ...

Cattanés also notes in relation to the carnival plays, "Avec ces pièces, Hans Sachs est le maître incontesté de la scène comique au XVI siècle."

18 Genée, 75

19 Ernst Karl Lützelberger, *Hans sachs, Sein Leben und Seine Dichtung* (Nürnberg, 1891), 17. "Ein solches Gedicht, von einem Schumacher verfasst, müsste grosses Aufsenhen erregen, und es verbreitet sich schnell im Volke durch ganz Deutschland. Der Missbrauch, welcher von Seiten der Geistlichen mit dem Glauben der Christen getrieben wurde, war darin mit einer Sachkenntnis, mit einer Wortfülle geschildert die uns heute noch staunen macht . . ."

20 Lützelberger, 22.

21 Genée, 103.

22 The interests of Master Sachs seemed not to be confined to any special area. We find *The Golden Ass of Apuleius*, books on anatomy, chronicles, the Bible, sermons, poetry (his own as well as others'), Aesop's Fables, histories, Homer, Herodotus, Petrarch, Boccaccio, Ovid, books on natural sciences etc., in the collection of this remarkable cobbler-poet. For a complete listing of Hans Sachs's inventory see: Emil Weller, *Hans Sachs und seine Dichtungen. Eine Bibliographie* (Neudruck der Ausgabe von 1868, Wiesbaden, 1966).

23 "Weil mich das Alter hart vexirt
Mich drückt beschwert und carcerirt . . ."

24 K. Trautmann cites clearly the influence of the *commedia dell'arte* on German theater in "Italienische schauspieles am bayrischen Hofe," Jahrbuch für Münchener Geschichte, I (1881), 225. In this study Trautmann mentions the popularity of the *Zanni* and *Pantalone* in Germany as deduced from the fact that they are the most prominent in the frescos at Schloss Trausnitz where they are portrayed with the Doctor, the Captain, and the lovers grouped about them. For a discussion of the scenarios, their location, and masks, see K. M. Lea, *Italian Popular Comedy, A Study of the commedia dell'arte* (Oxford, 1934), 129. See also Randall W. Listerman, *The Interludes (Los Pasos) by Lope Rueda* (Ottawa, 1988), 16.

25 Albert Köster, *Die Meistersingerbühne des sechzehten Jahrhunderts* (Halle, 1920), 6.

26 Köster, 8.

27 Köster, 53: ". . . gelegentlich Feuer und Rauch, ausgeteilte Prügel und Blutvergiessen . . ."

28 Genée, 346.

29 Hans Knudsen, *Deutsche Theatergeschichte* (Stuttgart, 1970), 71. "Die typischen Gestalten bei Hans Sachs dienen zur theatralischen Sichtbar-machung allgemeinmenschlicher Schwächen, aber so, dass die Einzel-merkmale sie doch individuell unterschiedlich erscheinen lassen."

30 Geiger, 266. "Hans Sachs qualifiziert die Wieber-scherzhaft-als ein übel, eine Plage, mit der man eben rechnen müsse, weil sie nun einmal da seien . . ."

BIBLIOGRAPHY

Arrowsmith, William and Roger Shattuck, eds. *The Craft and Context of Translation*. Austin, 1961.

Bakhtin, Mikhail. *Rabelais and His World*. Cambridge, 1985.

Beare, M. "Hans Sachs MSS. An Account of Their Discovery and Present Locations." *Modern Language Review* 52 (1957), 50–62.

Beecher, Donald A. and Massimo Ciavollela, eds. *Comparative Critical Approaches to Renaissance Comedy*. Ottawa, 1986.

Bristol, Michael. *Carnival and Theater*. New York, 1985.

Catholy, Eckehard. *Fastnachtspiel*. Stuttgart: J. B. Metzlersche Verlagsbuchhandlung, 1966.

Cattanés, Hélène. *Les Fastnachtsspiele de Hans Sachs*. Strassbourg, 1923.

Geiger, Eugen. *Hans Sachs als Dichter in Seinen Fastnachtsspielen*. Halle, 1904.

Genée, Rudolph. *Hans Sachs und seine Zeit*. Leipzig, 1894.

Goetze, Edmund. *Sämtliche Fastnachtsspiele von Hans Sachs in chronologischen Ordnung*. Halle, 1880.

Keller, Adalbert. *Fastnachtsspiele* II. Stuttgart, 1858.

Kluge, Friedrich. *Etymologisches Worterbuch der deutschen Sprache*. Berlin, 1967.

Knudsen, Hans. *Deutsche Theatergeschichte*. Stuttgart, 1970.

Könneker, Barbara. *Hans Sachs*. Stuttgart, 1971.

Köster, Albert. *Die Meistersingerbühne des sechsehnten Jahrhunderts*. Halle, 1921.

Lea, Kathleen M. *Italian Popular Comedy*. Oxford, 1934.

Listerman, Randall. "The Boccaccian Influence in the Dramatic Craftsmanship of Hans Sachs." *University of Dayton Review* 10 (1983), 99–105.

——————— . *The Interludes of Lope de Ruede*. Ottawa, 1988.

Lusky, G. F. "The Structure of Hans Sachs' *Fastnachtsspiele* in Relation to Their Place of Performance." *Journal of English and German Philology* 26 (1927), 521–40.

Lutzelberger, Karl Ernst. *Hans Sachs, sein Leben und seine Dichtung*. Nuremberg, 1891.

Rudwin, Maximilian J. *The Origin of the German Carnival Comedy*. New York, 1920.

Salinger, Leo. *Shakespeare and the Traditions of Comedy*. Cambridge, 1974.

Sobel, Eli. "Martin Luther and Hans Sachs." *Michigan Germanic Studies* (1984), 129–41.

Trautmann, K. *Jahrbuch für Münchener Geschichte* I. Munich, 1881.

Wackernagel, Wilhelm. *Geschichte der deutsche Literatur*. Basel, 1848.

Weller, Emil. *Hans Sachs und seine Dichtung. Eine Bibliographie*. Wiesbaden, 1966.

Wernicke, Siegfried. *Die Prosadialoge des Hans Sachs*. Berlin, 1913.

Hans Sachs

Nine Carnival Plays

(Fastnachtsspiele)

The Nose-Dance[1]

(1550)

A Carnival Play

The Mayor
The Milkman
Heinz Flail[2]
Eberlein Hunting-horn
Miser

Herman Brainless
Vail Pig-pen
Kunz Small-snout
Freddie Dungheap

(The Mayor enters carrying his staff and some prizes.
He addresses the assembled farmers.)

MAYOR: Alright everybody. Your attention please! Over here. Turn around! I have an announcement. All you farmers know good ol' cousin Gunker from Rebenstein. Why he owns most of the town. Well, he was nice enough to send us these three prizes you see hangin' here on this stick. Yep, it's all for our Nose-Dance celebration. Look here at these prizes: a box of snuff, a stick nose-picker, and a crown. There's a prize here for the three biggest noses we can find. The biggest of all gets the crown and will be our King of the Nose-Dance. The second biggest gets the snuff. The third place schnozzle will receive the nose-picker. So that everybody gets a chance to prove his point, let each and all pass before me. I'll be the judge. Let's see who measures up for the Nose-Dance. Don't be shy. Step right up single file so I can judge each nose with the measuring cup and ruler. Each contestant announce his name so we'll be able to recognize you.

(The Milkman steps out.)

MILKMAN: Mr. Mayor, I'm the milkman and my father was the manure man. He's the one who gave me this great nose that's so big I can't even see around it. Yep, it's always wet as a bathtub. If I press together here with two fingers — see there! I offer you lots of drops! It'll give me a whole handful if I want. Usually I just throw the stuff away and what a sound it makes — just like a frog hittin' the floor. Mr. Mayor, don't you think I deserve the prize?

(The Mayor measures with the cup.)

MAYOR: Now wait a minute. Let your neighbors have their chance too. I'll decide who gets the prize. Go over there and wait a spell.

(Heinz Flail steps out.)

HEINZ: Mr. Mayor, I'm Heinz Flail. My nose is crooked as a tree root. It's warty, knotty, and gnarled. Right here in the middle it's uneven like a fool's and twice as slippery. Look how long and thick it is. Couldn't lick a plate if I wanted to. I hope none of the other fellers get mad, but I'm gonna lead the Nose-Dance and win the crown. Because this nose knows best.

(The Mayor measures and speaks.)

MAYOR: Go over there and stand next to the milkman. Who knows who has the best? There are so many big noses over there yet!

(Everlein Hunting-horn steps out.)

EBERLEIN: Mr. Mayor, I'm Eberlein Hunting-horn. I too have a beaut of a bass horn. It hangs down over my mouth and makes me snore like a sick horse. It sure wakes up the wife and kids when I'm sleepin' at night. I'm afraid there's no remedy for me or the horse! See how knotty and crooked it is. Ha! Looks just like our out-house. With this ol' log all the rest look like pimples. Isn't that a fact, Mr. Mayor?

MAYOR: Go over there and take your place alongside those two. You triple the stakes. No pig could beat you.

(The Miser steps out.)

MISER: I'm the miser who lives over there on Wine Street. Mr. Mayor, look at my nose. Just look how squatty, knotty, clodded, and lumpy — just like a whore's rear. See it's even got corners just like that tower over there. Whoever sees these twin towers dies laughing. Although mother's was even bigger. I know I'll win the snuff as a prize. But, I really want the crown and to be King of the Nose-Dance. Come on, Mr. Mayor. Admit it, I've got the best one.

(The Mayor measures and speaks.)

MAYOR: Ja! But go over there and stand with the others and form a line and dance with them in time to the music.

(Herman Brainless steps out.)

HERMAN: Mr. Mayor, I'm known as Herman Brainless. Take a look at this nose — long and big. It makes a bow and there in the middle it's all humpy. See, it's full of veins — swollen and bony. It's stronger too than all the rest of the noses here. What a bottle-cork! It's bigger'n your hand above and below. So I'm the winner of he Nose-Dance, aren't I? Our plowman over there even bet on me.

MAYOR: Go over and wait your chance. Yours is not the only nose here. The others aren't exactly small.

(Vail Pig-pen steps out.)

VAIL: Mr. Mayor, I'm Vail Pig-pen. How do you like this cornet? It must be at least a span in length. It roars up like a fire from my face and far surpasses anyone here. See right here on the end? It's got a red club hard as copper. I've got to win one of the prizes. Why, when my wife gets in bed with me, there's no room for her. Now what do you think, Mr. Mayor?

(Mayor measures and speaks.)

MAYOR: Well, go over there and stand in line. You'll see soon enough who the winner is. But you do beat any sow I've ever seen.

(Kunz steps out.)

KUNZ: Mr. Mayor, my name is Kunz Small-snout. See this nose? Plump, wide, and short. When I move my nostrils like this, they spread out like pig sties. Whenever I blow this horn, every man, woman, and child — from near and far — knows and respects me. I also have long prickly, shaggy hairs growing out here. these ravelings are long enough to braid. It's not a long nose. But look at the thickness.

MAYOR: Alright. Go stand in line with the others. Let me measure first. Yep, thick as a lance is long.

(Freddie Dung-heap enters.)

FREDDIE: Mr. Mayor, I'm Dung-heap. I'm not much good at dancing so I probably can't take first prize. You see when I was a kid I really took it in the nose. An ol' sow bit it off while mother was working in the dung-pile. So that's why I got this li'l stump that looks like half a fist. Flat and square that's for sure, but it can hold two shovel-fulls at all times. Anyway, I'm hoping to win the nose-picker. In all my life, I've never had a picker. Mr. Mayor, think it over. I'll send you a summer supply of beans if only I could get that picker!

(Mayor measures and speaks.)

MAYOR: Go over and stand next to the others. It'll be hard to say what you'll win with your nose.

(The Mayor speaks to all the farmers.)

MAYOR: Well, is this it? Isn't there somebody else from town? We need more people for the Nose-Dance.

(He looks around at all of the spectators and speaks again.)

MAYOR: Now listen one and all. Farmers, townies, rich and poor, men and women, boys and girls, and all of you in between, if you've got a gifted snout, then step forward. The Nose-Dance makes us all the same, and the prizes are still open. If you are due one, step out now. No objections later.

(The Mayor looks all around and continues.)

MAYOR: Doesn't anybody want to step forward? I know there's still somebody who wants to dance. Somebody still wants to win the crown and be chosen Nose-King and represent all of the big noses. It's a big honor — but as nobody else is coming forward let the parade of noses begin.

HERMAN: Ach! Mr. Mayor. You stand with us too. You've got a beautiful schnoz. It would scare anybody. Just half of it is enough to qualify you. You lead us in the procession. Nobody will stop you.

MAYOR: Well, if that's your pleasure. I'll be happy to lead off. You drunks over there. Strike up the music.

*(They all join hands and dance around.
Then the Mayor speaks.)*

MAYOR: All you farmers now stand together! Let everybody inspect each other. And whoever during the Nose-Dance wins the crown, I'll do the honor. And no complaints from the losers.

*(The Mayor studies one after another and
then speaks to two farmers.)*

MAYOR: I'm afraid you two are about the same. Damn it! They're all runny!

(The Mayor measures another.)

MAYOR: Ja! You've got the over-all size. At least by a thick inch.

(The Mayor takes the crown.)

MAYOR: If the truth is known, all of you here at the Nose-Dance are deserving of winning the crown. You're almost equal. But we've only got one crown. So, I hereby crown Heinz Flail from Halbertown. He won fair and square.

(The Mayor puts the crown on Heinz, who stands next to the mayor. The others gather around.)

EBERLEIN: No sir, Mr. Mayor. I don't agree with your choice. I think my nose is bigger, why it's bigger than any three. Don't you think of all those in the Nose-Dance, I shoulda won the crown? How could you overlook me? My heart is almost breaking since you crowned that jack-ass. Now he'll just scorn and taunt us. Can't you find another king?

KUNZ: Look who's talkin'. No need for you to be flaunting your nose. Any pig leaves you far behind. What do you think? We don't have any noses? Look around at all of us. You can't see anybody on this platform who wouldn't like to be king. I would. Don't you think my nose is worthy?

EBERLEIN: Oh sure. It hangs down to the middle of your face. Just like an outhouse on the side of a hill. I would be happy to bow down to that schnoz.

VAIL: Well, there can only be one king. Heinz is as good as another. Let him lead us over to the tavern for some cool wine. We'll be his court and have a good ol' time.

MISER: Well, I really can't accept this either. All of my family — grandparents to female cousins — have knotty and ugly noses. Now I'll be the laughing stock of everybody in the parish. I must be the biggest fool to think the reputation of my nose now lies in dirt. Everybody will scorn and laugh at me.

MAYOR: Farmers and friends, what does it matter about the crown? Are you going to fight over this? Are you the biggest of fools? On Sunday somebody else can win. Let the crown stay for today with the king. Let's go over and get a pig for the roasting. Let's celebrate. Give in and quit arguing. Let's not seem ungrateful to the landlord.

FREDDIE: Well, I don't want to start a fight, but I'll say this. When I was younger I made sure my nose got respect. I would have beaten all of you. Now my poor nose — I'm so ashamed!

HERMAN: Dear neighbors, don't be sad and ill-tempered. Let the king keep his honor. Let's spend the day in peace and joy. Whoever wants to do this, raise your hand! Ah-hah. Majority wins!

KUNZ: Ja! Whoever starts a fight here gets ousted from the dance. We'll give him a crown he'll remember the rest of his life. Let the king remain just as the mayor said.

MILKMAN: No! I can't stand it! I'll fight him myself. Here are three of us who'll stand the whole town. We've all three got bigger noses than him. Let's fight for the crown. Whatya' want us to do? Stick our noses in an old lady's rear? You want us to stand around ashamed? You want us just to leave after we've told everybody who we are? I say take the crown and the prizes. Alright, then, we'll split the crown with him.

MISER: Ja! Milkman, I'm with you. What are we three just to walk away in shame? Nobody leaves this platform until the Nose-King lets go of his crown and blood is running from his muzzle. He isn't walking away from here with that crown. Let's tear him to pieces.

HEINZ: Mr. Mayor. So be it. I must defend myself. Hold my crown for a minute. I'll do a little dance with them if they want. We can settle the knottiest and gnarledest with blood. And soul stomping on the ground.

(Heinz furiously wipes his nose.)

HEINZ: Pig-shit! I've got the sniffles! Snffff! Sniff-sniff!! If you don't want to give me the crown, I'll take all three of you on. I'll hold my honor up no matter what. Come on! Don't lag behind each other!

MAYOR: Farmers. Please let's have peace. For the love of money, body and soul. Don't move or I swear, by Jove, I'll strike too.

(The farmers start to push and hit one another.)

MAYOR: Ladies, gentlemen, and landowner, the Nose-Dance is canceled for today on account of the fight you see. I'll keep the crown and other prizes too. But come back on Sunday and we'll end our dance. And, if by chance, you have a good friend, neighbor, or acquaintance, an uncle or relative who also is nose-gifted, then bring them here. Let's make the line even longer 'cuz that's our wish. A pastime full of cheer and humor is the best way for a carnival play. Put away malice and meanness. Have a good night and a good night bids you all — Hans Sachs.

The Stolen Bacon

(1551)

A Carnival Play

Hans the village priest   Heinz Knoll, a farmer
Hermann Doll, the miserly farmer   Kunz Droll, a farmer

(*Heinz Knoll enters, speaking to himself.*)

HEINZ: Ohhhh. Oh my head. Oh whatta headache. I can barely stand
on my own two feet. The whole night drinking. Hic. No wonder
I staggered home. All that sausage made me so thirsty I drank
all the more. Oh-well. At carnival time everybody drinks, gets
happy, and like me — gets a little foggy in the head.

(*Kunz Droll, the other farmer, enters.*)

KUNZ: A very fine mornin' to you Heinz Knoll.

HEINZ: Thank you, neighbor Kunz Droll.

KUNZ: Why, you look like you haven't slept a wink.

HEINZ: You're right. Me and the priest spent the whole night drinkin'.
The roosters were crowin' when I staggered home.

KUNZ: My God! Was it that late?

HEINZ: Yep, and I was loaded too.

KUNZ: Yeah, I can see now you really were. Hope you helped the
priest eat some of the big sausage he had on hand. Hey, wait!
I almost forgot. Did you hear tell that two days ago Hermann
butchered his big ol' sow? I heard four fingers thick of bacon.

HEINZ: D'ya get any from him?

KUNZ: Naw. And I give him some of mine every year. But him?
Give me sausage? Never.

HEINZ: He's a skinflint. He's the biggest cow pie around. Every year
we have him over to our butchering party and he ain't never let
me even try an ear from his sow. He's a cheapskate. Wurst for

wurst — that's what the ol' proverb says. And by God, he's heard it often from me too. But he don't listen.

KUNZ: Look, how about you and me — just us two — tonight, going over there and helpin' ourselves to some of his bacon? We'll fix him, the ol' tightwad.

HEINZ: Often thought about it. How do we do it?

KUNZ: Here's a plan. I'll just go over and ask him to lend me somethin'. In the meantime, while I'm talkin' with him, you sneak around back to his smokehouse. Grab that bacon right clean outta the barrel where that ol' sow is sittin' there soakin' in salt. Haul that bacon up and you just sashay on home. You and me — we'll have it gone in no time.

HEINZ: All hell's gonna break loose if he finds out.

KUNZ: Well, let's just cook up a plan to save our skins. Hmmm. Say, if the priest joined us, we'd have good protection. He wouldn't let us get in trouble; and besides, you know how he likes a good joke. He's helped us pull off some humdingers over the years.

HEINZ: Yeah. You're right, Kunz. He sure has. And, the priest knows what a tight ass Hermann is, too.

KUNZ: So what'ya waitin' for? Let's go. Tonight when people are lightin' their lamps, we'll be lickin' our chops.

(The two exit. Hermann Doll, the miserly farmer,
enters, speaking to himself.)

HERMANN: Oh, she's so plump and lardy. Now I've got that fat pig all butchered and soakin' in the salt. I fed her good and it shows — she's a biggie. Can't wait to gnaw on those bones. The butcher wasn't thinking when he made these long wursts. Why he coulda made three instead of the two he rolled out. That ol' sow was packed so full he coulda served me up half a bacon-loaf more, if he wanted. Sure, then I coulda given several wursts to my neighbors. I want to give some, but it sure would be nice to keep all the sausages just for me. I could eat the whole pig by myself. If I share, then I won't have enough for carnival. So why share?

(Kunz Droll enters.)

KUNZ: Good-evening, Hermann Doll.

HERMANN: To you too, dear Kunz. What brings you over here so late?

KUNZ: Oh, my farm-hand busted my axe handle. And I myself broke my flail and I can't finish my threshin'. I was hopin' to finish up

come mornin'. Would you mind lendin' me yours? Please. Just
your spares.

HERMANN: Yeah. Alright. I'll lend 'em. But watch out you don't
go bustin' mine too. And two days only. I can't lend them any
longer.

KUNZ: Say, old friend, let's grill a couple of those bratwursts. Let me
see how they taste. Boy, have you got sausages hangin' everywhere.

HERMANN: Nope, nope. No can do. You know my wife would moan
and groan at me. I'd lose every bit of her favor and grace.

KUNZ: Come on. She's takin' a bath. Whatya think your wife can
possibly say?

HERMANN: Can't do it. Just two days ago she counted the whole
bunch. I can't go against her. You know what she's like. Here
now. Come on take the flail. Here's the axe-handle too.

(*Both exit. Heinz Knoll and Kunz Droll enter and Kunz is speaking.*)

KUNZ: Knoll did you get it? Did you? The bacon?

HEINZ: Oh! It was close. I almost got caught. But, I got it home safe
and sound.

KUNZ: What should we do with the bacon now?

HEINZ: Let's take it over to the rectory. I told the priest early this
morning all about our plan. God, did he laugh! He wants to be
in on the trick. Fact is, he said he would trick ol' Hermann into
confessin' he stole his own bacon himself. Uh-uh. Quiet. Here
comes Hermann now. Look at him. He's cryin' tears bigger that
eggs.

(*Hermann enters dejectedly.*)

HEINZ: Hey, hey. What's this? Why so sad?

HERMANN: Oh, oh, oh. I'm miserable, my dear neighbors. Oh no.
I've lost my best bacon today.

KUNZ: Ha-ha-ha! Oh, I have to laugh. I can't believe you Hermann.
If you had lost it, you'd be swearin' up a storm.

HERMANN: Naw, it's true. Right this afternoon, behind closed door.
I even had the door bolted. No, my bacon has really been stolen.
It's true.

KUNZ: Listen to him. You probably stole it yourself, 'cuz nobody
coulda ever gotten inside there. You robbed it yourself so you
could give it to your girlfriend Striegel Christen.

HERMANN: Oh, Lordy! Don't even think that name. You'll drive me crazy. Oh, God, help me get my bacon back, huh? Oh, my life is gonna be manure. My wife is gonna beat me and then rip me apart. She's gonna peck me raw like a fat hen.

HEINZ: Hey, look there. The priest is comin' across the threshin' floor leadin' a black cow.

PRIEST: Good tidings, my neighbors. What's up? Town meeting?

HERMANN: Oh, dear Sir, why shouldn't I complain? Right now in the early evening I lost my bacon. I mean it's been stolen. Yes, stolen! Please, Sir, couldn't I ask you to do some of you black magic? Use your hocus-pocus to bring that sow thief to justice. Make him give me back my beloved bacon.

PRIEST: Dear Hermann. Of course, I can. And indeed I shall. Via my magic prowess and art, I shall indicate who is guilty of stealing your bacon.

HERMANN: Sir! Do it! Before it's too late, before the thief hears tell about it. I want that bacon away from that thief no matter who he is.

PRIEST: If I am to indicate, however, who the thief is, then I must use my art. Notice, I have in my hand a branch from a ginger plant. I shall place the branch down, utter my imploring oath and blessing; and then each person takes some. He who can eat his portion without a trace of bitterness is summarily free of guilt of the theft. But, he who finds the ginger leaf to be bitter as gall, then he indeed is the bacon thief. Hermann, if you wish, we can start the magic procedure. Obviously, I can not arrange the preparations for *gratis*, as they say. Do give me five dollars so I can initiate the procedure to determine whether your bacon still wants to belong to you.

HERMANN: Oh! Oh, I don't have any money on me, dear priest. I buried some in the garden, though, so my wife wouldn't find it. I'll go right now and dig it up. All five dollars, just like you said. Could you hold the trick for just a moment?

PRIEST: I summon you back as soon as possible. And I summon your neighbors, together with you, to meet in the churchyard by the wall. There we shall test all those present if my calculations do not fail me.

(Hermann runs off stage.)

HEINZ: Father, how will this work?

(The Priest lays the ginger branch on the ground.)

PRIEST: Heinz Knoll, look here. On these three leaves I have put
     sugar. The first one, I'll pick. You, Heinz, pick this one here.
     And you, Kunz, take this third one. The leaf on the inside is
     for Hermann. See, it's covered with aloe powder and dogshit.
     I've sprinkled sugar on top so Hermann will be fooled. He won't
     be able to eat this little morsel. With his gagging he'll proclaim
     loud and clear — even he will believe — that he himself is the bacon
     thief. He stole it to give to his little girlfriend Striegel. He'll be
     so confused — and you be very serious about his theft — that we'll
     pull the thing off. We'll cover our trick and probably scare some
     more money out of him. Then, by God, let's go get that bacon
     and heave to, keeping quiet among us with appropriate God-like
     stillness and honor.

HEINZ: Hold it down! Listen! Here comes Hermann running the
     whole way back.

(Hermann Doll runs on stage, handing money to the Priest.)

HERMANN: Here they are, Father. Five dollars fresh from the earth
     so's to catch that thief. And here's another fiver just to make sure
     you really try hard to make the magic work.

(The Priest picks up the ginger plant.)

PRIEST: Now hear ye, hear ye the oath:
          In Narribus phantastibus
          Nequamque et in diebibus
          Hanges in galgare Fane
          Rabiquenagare pame[1]
     Now all of you sit down next to each other. Each one of you take
     a leaf of ginger, my children. He who is able to chew and then
     swallow the leaf is completely innocent of the bacon theft. But
     he who is unable to swallow the leaf suffers the revenge of the
     stolen bacon. He then will be guilty and he is the one who has
     committed the theft. In order to test the magic, I will be the first
     to submit myself to the test.

(The Priest eats the leaf.)

HERMANN: Oh Sir! I never said I suspected you. You didn't need to
     draw a leaf.

HEINZ: Huh! Maybe you want me not to draw too. I'll just pass.

HERMANN: No, go on Heinz. Draw a leaf. If you're innocent you will
     chew it and then swallow it.

(Heinz picks out a leaf and swallows it.)

HEINZ: Now you see. I'm innocent.

HERMANN: Kunz, go on, it's your turn now.

KUNZ: Alright, alright. I'll do it . . . if I have to. But I'm innocent, I tell you. And it bothers me that you make me draw to prove I'm not the thief.

PRIEST: Ach! Nobody gets off from anything that might keep this good man from getting his bacon back.

(Kunz Droll takes a leaf and eats it.)

KUNZ: There. You see. I'm innocent. Now, go ahead and you take the fourth leaf and let's see if you're innocent.

(Hermann Doll draws the leaf.)

HERMANN: Of course, I will draw. Fearlessly. I know that I am innocent.

(Hermann Doll throws the leaf in his mouth and grimaces.)

PRIEST: I think the thief is about to be revealed. It seems Hermann is having trouble swallowing his leaf.

(Hermann Doll spits everything out.)

HERMANN: My God, my muzzle stings. Yuk! God, that's bitter. My whole body belches and trembles. How my eyes water. I'll be the thief my life-long. I can't swallow that. It tastes like dogshit! Yuk. It strikes me clear to my heart. Oh God, look out, I'm going to be sick. I've gotta heave.

(Kunz Droll grabs him.)

KUNZ: Ah-hah! Not so fast you old scoundrel. What kind of a game you playing on us? You steal your own bacon and then go around accusin' honest folks. You took that bacon yourself to give it as a love gift. I oughta thrash you with a wood wedge 'til your sins show through.

HEINZ: No, wait a minute, Kunz. I can't let you do that. Let's hit him really hard. Let's tell his wife. Let's tell her he took the bacon so's to give it to his little Striegel Christen. Ah yes. Ha-ha. She'll go stark-ravin' mad. She'll start by pullin' out his beard and movin' down. You couldn't give him worse punishment.

(Hermann Doll raises both hands straight up.)

HERMANN: Oh! Oh . . . dear neighbors, please. Be still. Be quiet. Don't turn me in. I couldn't ever go home. Whatever you say, I can't deny it. The magic tells the story. I've stolen many things in my day, but I've always remembered about them too! If I've stolen the bacon from myself, I sure can't recall how, where or when I did it. And for the life of me I know I can't remember if I gave the bacon to Christen. But you better believe my wife would believe it. If you just say one thing about Striegel Christen she'll hound me every day 'til eternity. Oh dear me. If wife ever found out that Striegel had our bacon — oh God, I'd be white hot tortured. Please, I beg you. Don't ruin my marriage.

PRIEST: His marriage is above evil revenge, my brothers. I understand! Accordingly, let us put things right; but also in a manner that suits our honor. We forgive you for everything. Nevertheless, you must do penance and you must compensate for the false accusation. I would say a guilder[2] should be an adequate amount to cover a few drinks, should we choose to imbibe. And perhaps twenty bratwursts would change our ill-humor to joy and forgiveness.

HERMANN: Yes, yes. Of course, I'll give you two guilders. But my wife counts all the bratwursts, and she knows when even a slice is missing. Oh please, she knows if I even touch one. But listen, I'll go right now to fetch the two buried guilders from the garden. Father, I'll bring 'em right to your house. But please, won't you please tell wife that a thief climbed through the window and stole that bacon?

PRIEST: Go my son. Of course, all of us want to and will help you.

(Hermann runs off.)

PRIEST: Well once in a while you have to trick the apes and punish stingy misers. Hard wood has to be split with maul and wedge, or it stays rock hard a lifetime. The opportunity turned out well for us. Come on now. Let's go simmer and roast our prize. We'll have several rounds on Hermann the miser.

You know, actually, no good-hearted person could wish him evil. So come on, let's go over to the rectory courtyard and drink 'til daybreak. Let Hermann go gnaw on bones because he can't enjoy goodness. He buries and ruins it. So he buries his money, eh? Well, for every stingy person there should be a spender, so that the tightwad's money sack doesn't get too big — that's what wishes Hans Sachs.

The Calf-Hatching

(1551)

A Carnival Play

Hans, farmer   Gretta, farmer's wife
The village priest

(The farmer's wife enters, speaking to herself.)

GRETTA: Ach, woe is me! What can a poor body do? My husband
is so sloppy. Such a messy, lazy, good-for-nothing slob. He's
so lazy I can't even get him out of bed. He lies there the whole
night snoring like an old nag. I tell him — get up early and help
me before I go to town. The milk and eggs won't sell themselves.
I'm up at the crack of dawn. Here I am out here in the cold
milking the cow. I'm all set to go and that loafer still isn't up.
Even the rooster can't wake him up. I'll go see if I can roust him
out of bed to look after the farm while I'm gone.

(The farmer enters, yawning and scratching his head.)

HANS: Good morning, old girl! How come you're up so early?

GRETTA: In the devil's name! I was comin' right now to give that
thick-skinned carcass of yours some good whacks.

HANS: Ach. Dear Gretta, you make me laugh. It's so early. Not even
the hens or roosters are up. Why should I be?

GRETTA: You lazy, good-for-nothing! They would have hung you long
ago, if it weren't for me. Just you tell me, what am I going to do
with you? Just tell me!

HANS: Oh now. Come on and be still, I'm not so bad. Go and bring
us lots of money from the market. I'll stay home and take care of
the place. I'll do some sweeping and heat the stove. I can do all
that just as good as you.

GRETTA: Then put the meat and the herbs on the table. And don't

forget, when the mayor blows his horn it's time to put the pig
and the cow out to pasture. And tidy up this place too. We'll eat
when I get back from market.

HANS: I'll not forget a thing. I'll do everything just like you say.

GRETTA: We'll see. When I get home, your housekeeping better be
good or your head will pay. If anything goes wrong . . .

(*The farmer's wife exits. Hans remains speaking after her.*)

HANS: Go on! Go on. There's nothing to worry about . . . nothing.
Gosh, it sure is early in the morning. Maybe I'll make a fire and
sit for a spell. Or . . . maybe I'll just go back to bed and rest
for an hour or so. I'll sleep 'til the major blows his horn. Then
I'll let the old sow and cow out to pasture. Gosh, it's still just
daybreak. It's so early. So early.

(*The farmer exits. Waits. Then runs back on stage.*)

HANS: Oh my dead body! Oh, oh. Oh, no, I overslept. Oh wife will
scream bloody murder. The mayor has blown his horn and my
cow is still in the barn. I'll pay for this. Pig shit! I forgot the
herb sauce. There it is crackling and gushing on the fire. What's
it doing over there?

(*The farmer exits. Gretta enters carrying a bundle.*)

GRETTA: Whew! Well, I've been to town. Wonder how that vermin
kept house while I was gone? Was there ever such a husband?
Like always he probably didn't do half what I told him to. Better
get on home to see how bad things are. I might just as well let
my luck go on a pilgrimage because he'll never change no matter
what. I could strike him dead and the fool wouldn't know he's
dead. Glad I had that drink of wine in town. This is all up-hill.
Well, almost home and it seems not a minute too late.

(*Gretta exits. Hans enters scratching his head.*)

HANS: Oh dear God! I'm some cook! The soup boiled all over the
stove. The cat was sitting on the back porch eating the meat. But,
I fixed him. Ripped his gut right open and took it back!

Oh these herbs are all burnt on this side and look rotten here
on the other. Uh-oh. When wife comes home, she'll blister my
hide. Oh well. I can be happy about my pig, the calf and the cow.
I know they're happy. Right there in our little garden where I put
them. It's gettin' noon-day, maybe I better put them back in the
barn before wife gets home from town.

(The farmer exits but returns hurriedly saying sadly.)

HANS: Oh no! The roof will fall on me now! I go out in the garden, and what do I see? My calf fell in the well and drowned! Oh no. Wife wanted to sell that calf to get a new coat. Oh that's only the half of it. What's to become of me now? How can I explain this? She'll skin me alive. I won't wait in the house for her. She'll hang me up on a hook. Oh woe is me. How my life turns topsy-turvy. How, oh how, can I get another calf? Hey, wait. Wait! Hens and geese just brood 'em out of eggs. Why sure. They just sit on the eggs a couple of days and hatch their youngin's out. Sure. I'll just hatch me a calf out of cheese. I'll just get some straw and let magic do the rest. I'll just put this cheese here in the barrel and throw some herbs on top. No doubt about it. You can brood a calf from cheese. Guess I'll hatch 'em over here in the shade. Even if someone talks to me, I won't pay no mind, I'll just keep broodin' and hatchin' my calf. I'm out of trouble now.

(Gretta enters mumbling to herself.)

GRETTA: Well! Back from town and the devil took that husband of mine. I yelled all over for him. No coals in the fire, meat gone, the soup pot broken, the herbs burnt to a crisp, soup swimming all over the oven, dead-drowned calf in the garden. What next? My fool go hang himself? No wonder I cuss. Hell. I'll go look for some herbs.

(Gretta exits and re-enters yelling.)

GRETTA: Hans! Hans!

(Gretta sees Hans sitting in the barrel.)

GRETTA: You idiot! What are you doing?

(Hans replies like goose.)

HANS: Eh! Eh!
GRETTA: You're crushing the herbs.
HANS: Eh! Eh! Pff! Pff!
GRETTA: How did you ruin the meat and herbs? The cat is dead, the calf is drowned, and I was hoping you had gone and hung yourself.
HANS: Zisch! Zisch! Pff! Pff!

GRETTA: What? You dare heap scorn on top of all this damage? I'll make fillets out of you. I'll slice you as softly as your gut. I'll cram you into the ground.

(*Gretta rushes at Hans and he screams.*)

HANS: Pff! Pff!

GRETTA: You just wait. I'll get you out of there!

HANS: Eh! Eh! Pff! Pff!

GRETTA: Rascal! Get up! Go feed the sow!

HANS: Zisch! Zisch!

GRETTA: What are you doing? Are you crazy? Wait. Wait. I'll go fetch the priest. The dead calf made you go crazy.

HANS: Pff! Pff! Eh! Eh!

(*Gretta exits. The farmer stands up, picks up the cheese and looks at it, puts it down, and sits on top of it. Gretta returns with the priest.*)

GRETTA: Oh dear sir, please help me and save him. I went to market early this morning and when I returned home sweating, puffing, panting from the walk here, I find my husband sitting in this barrel in our herb patch. He acts like a looney cricket. Everything I ask him he just answers like a goose: Pff! Pff! Pff! Pff! And he swings his arms up and down like he was flapping his wings. I can't get a word out of him. I think he's gone crazy. Please help him, father. Try and bring him back.

(*The priest stares at Hans.*)

PRIEST: Ah, dear Gretta, I think it's a case of too much brandy. It went right to the top of his head.

GRETTA: No. He hasn't had a drop of brandy. He just drinks wine which he never gets enough of.

PRIEST: Let's see. Let's see here. I'll speak to him kindly. "Hello, my dear neighbor, Hans."

HANS: Eh! Ch! Pff! Pff!

PRIEST: You, you pffst at me, like a goose?

HANS: Oh! Ch! Pff! Pff!

PRIEST: Tell me, what have you gotten in your skull to make you like this?

HANS: Pff! Pff!

PRIEST: Tell me. Did a ghost get you? What's gotten into you? Where cometh such strange gestures?

HANS: Pff! Pff!

PRIEST: Can't you talk? Just nod. Is it black magic? Are you be-
witched? Are you robbed of your senses? Is this it? Nod your
head!

HANS: Pff! Pff!

(The priest turns to Gretta.)

PRIEST: Gretta, I can only presume that your husband is completely
possessed.

GRETTA: Help him. Drive out the evil spirits, father, and I'll repay
you.

PRIEST: Oh Gretta, it's easy for you to say "exorcise my husband";
and, of course, I can. But I really am not too inclined to do so
right now. Just look at him! See how roguish he looks. Spiteful,
secretive, sneaky. His eyes shine like cat eyes, and look how they
follow me. Maybe he'll hurt me. Maybe I should wait awhile.
The devil can be very powerful.

GRETTA: Ach! It's not that bad. Go on and exorcise him. Don't
worry, I'm standing right here beside you. Hans, you won't fight
when the priest drives out those evil spirits, will you?

HANS: Pff! Pff! Ch! Ch!

(The priest takes out a book and reads.)

PRIEST: I exorcise you to come out. Devil! Come out in the name of
every beggar's plague, by every priest's purity, by every whisper
and purring of a secret, by all true adulterers, by all young girls'
repentance. Yes, and also by all the spirituality of all humanity, by
all farmers' piety, by every jokster's accident, by all gone astray
Jews, by all pretty ladies' charm, by all beginners' patience, by
all shopkeepers' honest prices—by all of these things you must
come out. Come out of this man and get thee to the wildest part
of the Beimer Forest. Get thee gone!

HANS: Pff! Pff! Ch! Ch! Ch!

*(The priest throws a wooden chain around Hans' neck. Gretta
screams and falls behind the priest as both pull Hans
out of the barrel on top of them in a pile.)*

HANS: What? What are you doing here? You are taking me from my
kids. You horse nuts you! You really bring me honor and goods
now that you've pulled me from my brood. What do you think?
Nobody would find me back here? The devil take you both.

PRIEST: Hans, what in the world? Brooding?

(The farmer screams and points to the cheese.)

HANS: Calves! Calves! Look at them. That cheese is full of maggots.
See? Under, on top, behind, in front! All of them would be calves
if you hadn't pulled me from my brood!

PRIEST: Hans, I would like to know who, for heaven's sake, taught
you this art?

HANS: Who taught me? Fright, worry, and fear of my wife taught me.
That's who.

PRIEST: Oh come on! Tell us truly what made you attempt such a
stunt?

HANS: Of course, I will. If you won't hit me.

GRETTA: Alright. But I ought to knock you dead.

HANS: Where do I start my tale of woe? I fell asleep and didn't hear
the mayor blow his horn. So I didn't know when to let our cow
out to pasture. So I put him in the garden to eat. And while I
was cooking the calf fell in the well and drowned. I was really
sad then. And afraid too.

   Then I got the thought. Hens and geese brood their young
from only eggs. Cheese is kinda the same thing, so why not hatch
some calves the same way? So I just picked up this cheese and
perched on top of it. If you two hadn't come along, I woulda had
a real brood.

GRETTA: You imbecile! You're the biggest fool in the parish. Get
inside. Chop that wood, you lazy-bones. Get going or I'll give
you something for your dumb head. I'll get that calf out of your
hide yet.

PRIEST: Now, Gretta, you already promised you wouldn't hit him. So
leave him alone.

GRETTA: What? Do you want to make a laughing-stock out of me?
How can you stand up for such a moron? He plagues me all day
long with his lazy ways and unfinished chores.

HANS: Sir, you better not get mixed up in this. My wife will take aim
at your head if you start to pick a bone with her.

GRETTA: Shut up! Get in there! Chop!

PRIEST: Gretta, you really are an old nag. Don't treat your husband
like that.

HANS: Dear Sir, if you think her tongue is bad, you should see her
punches.

PRIEST: Gretta, Gretta. I've never seen such behavior as yours.

GRETTA: Ja! That's right. I never spare him any blows when he deserves them. Why should I let him off scot-free? I lock him in the closet and then sweep him out like a tree frog when I'm good and ready.

PRIEST: Oh Gretta! Shame on you. You are a disgrace to woman's name. It is the man who is supposed to be master in his house.

(*Gretta doubles her fists and goes toward the priest.*)

GRETTA: Hold your tongue, priest. And move along now. You have no more business here you stinking little run-about. Disappear from here or I'll give you a little blessing you won't soon forget.

(*The priest turns to leave.*)

PRIEST: I came here in peace and that's how I shall leave. But, I say in parting, you Gretta are the one possessed by the devil. You are the one in need of exorcism.

(*Gretta moves toward the priest.*)

GRETTA: Oh come on priest. Let's forgive and forget.

(*The priest runs away saying*)

PRIEST: No, no. Just let me go.

(*Gretta speaks to Hans.*)

GRETTA: Well, I'll be damned. And you, you good-for-nothing oaf, get in the house. Forget about the wood. I'd just have to feed you then. It's tit-for-tat. If the priest hadn't pulled you out of the barrel, you would still be brooding your cheese. I ought to shove it in your mouth. What's the use? Why get all steamed up and just hurt myself? I give up on you. Here, take this money and go over to the tavern and fetch us some wine. We might as well drink up the money I made at the market. Come on let's sit down and drink our wine. Let's forget all this hullabaloo and hassle and bring on some good times — so says Hans Sachs.

The Wife in the Well

(1552)

A Carnival Play

Steffano, the husband   Gitta, his wife
Anthony, Gitta's brother

(Steffano enters speaking to himself.)

STEFFANO: I've got some wife alright. Every night she loads me up
with wine and then walks me into bed. She didn't do that a year
ago. I can't say she gives me all this wine because she loves
me more. I'm afraid there's a trick or something going on here.
While I was lying in bed last night, I suddenly remembered her
and that Martin fellow over at the dance. They were sure having a
good time. I just acted as if I wasn't noticing them. But, I'll find
out. I'll find out tonight. I'll just pretend I have had too much to
drink with my brother. I'll let on I've drunk the whole barrel of
Rhine wine. Then just like always she'll lead me to bed. But I'll
just wait, watch, and see what she does. Ha! Look here. It's my
wife slithering up the walk now.

(Gitta, the wife, enters and speaks.)

GITTA: Steffano, where are you going? Wouldn't you like to stay
home?

STEFFANO: Oh, I'm just taking a walk over to my brother's house.

GITTA: Shame on you! Go on! You drunk! You won't come home
sober.

STEFFANO: *(Aside)* I won't have to wait long now.

(Steffano exits. Gitta remains speaking to herself.)

GITTA: So much the better if you come home drunk. Then I won't
have to fill you up. Every night I have to wait until you pass out

to let my lover in the house. Or sometimes we go to his place while my drunken fool husband lies there sleeping. He grunts and farts like a pig and how his putrid breath stinks. He dribbles like an old man—something that looks like pig slop. When I get back from my lover's I just lay down next to my sow and sleep until morning. I never worry that he'll suspect my lover because I get him so drunk every night he just passes out. Ha! Here he comes now staggering up. I think he is completely drunk.

STEFFANO: Wife, wife, wife. Oh. I'm really dead drunk.

GITTA: No need to shout it. I can see.

STEFFANO: Four b-b-barrels. F-F-Four barrels of Rhine wine down the hatch. Oh, boy, how I staggered home.

GITTA: Oh! Come on now lie down right away so the wine will run its course. Here, before you catch cold, lie down.

STEFFANO: Ja! The good old bed for me. Oh my head is whirling around like a whirligig. Everything is just whirling and swirling. Schwirling. Schwir—

(She leads him off-stage, re-enters speaking.)

GITTA: Now I've got my sow in his stall. Now I'll be on my merry way. Tonight I can be real certain he won't wake up. Around one or two o'clock he'll start reaching around in bed just to make sure I'm there. He'll think I've been there all along. This great trick has worked every time for the last six months. He's drunk and I'm delighted with my lover. He fills his gut, and I get mine filled too, and I'm lying if it isn't so.

(Gitta exits. Steffano enters.)

STEFFANO: Well, there she goes sneaking out. Off to her little boyfriend, just like I figured she was doing. She plied me with wine every night so she could run off with some scoundrel. Now I know! And I know just what to do. I'll lock her out. I'll bolt the door and sit here behind the shutter until she comes slinking back. I'll scare her so that I'll put an end to her whoring around. By Jove, she better start spending her nights with me. There she comes slinking along. Ha! Wonder what she'll say to a locked door.

(The wife enters, tries to open the door with a key.)

GITTA: I'll be a pig's corpse! The inner bolt is latched. Who did that? My husband must be awake. The devil put him up to it. But he was so drunk you coulda punched open a door with him. Let me see now. I don't want to be discovered. Maybe I can slide the bolt here with my knife. Ach. Won't work. It's better to just knock. I'll knock softly and maybe the maid will hear me before my husband. She'll let me in, and I can just slide right in before the cock crows.

(She knocks once or twice. Steffano speaks.)

STEFFANO: Wife, oh wife — your soft knocking is all in vain. You can't come in. Go away, go back from where you came! You'll never be with me again. Go show your piety elsewhere. Go throw your honor to the wind and get what you deserve. Go on! Quit knocking at my door.

GITTA: Oh dear friend. Please just open the door. Don't cause me any shame. You are so wrong to think I could dishonor you. No, no dear husband, you are so very wrong. Don't you want me by your side in bed? Don't you want me to cook for you? I just went over to the spinning-room to visit our god-parents. I was only sewing. Please open the door! Don't be stubborn. Don't make me scream!

STEFFANO: What? You're coming from our god-parents and the spinning room in the middle of the night? Where is your lantern, honorable wife?

GITTA: Husband, please. It went out. Look. Please open the door and let me in.

STEFFANO: Not tonight will I let you in. You can go sleep in jail and publicly proclaim your shame. Or go stand in the stockade. Go on now, you'll not get in here tonight.

GITTA: Do you want me to suffer blame and shame innocently? Alright. Then tonight I'll do something that will make you shamed and scorned by everybody on earth. Poor husband!

STEFFANO: What will you do, you evil old bag?

GITTA: Ha! You just watch me. You snake in the grass. I'll go drown myself in the well and then everyone will think you just let me drown. Ha! Then everyone will be out looking for you with my innocent blood on your hands. Everyone will curse you and speak evil of you. You'll have to leave home. What does it matter to me? I'm going to save my honor. You'll never see me alive. Oh God, I commend to Thee my soul. Keep me from eternal torment.

(She throws a stone in the well.)

STEFFANO: I heard a big ker-plunk out there. My wife must have fallen in the well. Oh dear, woe is me. To think that my hard words brought her to such an end. I'll run and see if I can still help my wife out of the well before she drowns. I'll win her back and heat her up with gifts and presents.

(The husband runs to the well. The wife quickly runs from around the house and locks the front door.)

GITTA: Now you are outside, and I am on the inside. Now I'll win the game. Now I'm calling the tunes and you'll be singing them. I'll bring you to your knees. I'll just sit here at the window and listen to see what that fool husband of mine is doing at the well. I really threw a large stone.

(The husband looks down the well and shouts.)

STEFFANO: Gitta! Gitta! Are you down there? Are you still alive? Are you dead? Answer me. Sit on the bucket and I'll pull you up. I'm not angry anymore, honest. I forgive you! Just still be alive!

(He scratches his head and speaks again.)

STEFFANO: She's drowned. I can't hear her. Let the whole world pity her. I can never be forgiven for this sin!

GITTA: You big fool! What are you doing out there mousing around the well? Haven't you had enough to drink already?

STEFFANO: Well in all my days, I never thought I'd hear my wife's voice again. I'll look in the house. Hey! The door's locked. Wife? Where are you?

GITTA: You lazy sow! Are you just coming home from drinking? Isn't it enough for you to drink from noonday on? Just like you to come staggering home at two o'clock in the morning.

STEFFANO: Open the door! Don't be so uncouth! You scared me to death! I thought you had jumped down the well.

GITTA: What are you prattling about? What well? You are hallucinating from your stupor.

STEFFANO: Just hold it down and open the door. Let me just go to bed.

GITTA: Ach! You drunken, good-for-nothing husband. You aren't getting in this house tonight. Go stay at the madhouse where you belong. Better not let the watchman catch you here, or you'll end up in jail with the other asses and scoundrels. Everybody knows,

even my brother Anthony, that all you do is drink all day and
night. You've ruined our marriage.

(Anthony, Gitta's brother, enters.)

ANTHONY: Brother-in-law, what are you screaming about at such
hours? Both of you go to bed. Let people sleep.

GITTA: Oh dear brother, let that husband of mine go to jail. Every
night he comes home late from drinking. While he is off drinking,
I'm all alone.

ANTHONY: Brother-in-law, that shouldn't be. You should stay home
and keep things all together. Don't go running off to the tavern
every night and then drag home drunk. Your friendships won't
suffer if you are honorable and up-standing.

STEFFANO: Look at her would you! I'm the one who should be complaining, not her. Dear brother-in-law, let me just tell you. Your
sister went sneaking out of the house tonight to go see her lover.
I got out of bed and closed and bolted the door. I locked your
sister out. When she finally came home, I wasn't going to let her
in the house. I wanted her to go moaning to her friends—then
they would know that she is whoring around. I just wanted to
scare her out of having affairs. That's all. I was protecting her
honor. But then she cooked up a trick by saying she was going
to drown herself. She threw a big stone down the well, and when
I heard the loud ker-plop I thought she actually jumped. I ran
lickety-split, sober as can be, to help her out of the well. In the
meanwhile, she snuck back in the house and locked me out. Just
like you find me now.

ANTHONY: Sister, sister, I don't like this one bit. What have you
done? You deserve a good thrashing.

GITTA: Dear brother, please listen to me. He's drunk and doesn't know
what he is even saying. He's not telling the truth. I never left
my house tonight. I'm inside and he's outside stumbling around
the well like a dumb fool. He's so drunk he can hardly stand.
He lets me go hungry and all my friends know it too. Oh I'm so
miserable! Take me home with you.

ANTHONY: Now we're getting to the bottom of this. I had no idea your
house was like this. So, you lay around day and night in a sloppy
stupor. Is my sister telling the truth? You know, I always thought
you were an honorable man. You always seemed up-standing. But
you're a good-for-nothing oaf. You deceived my sister and me.

STEFFANO: Your sister deceived me. I have not had a drop of wine all day long. Now she paints me out to be a drunkard. Ha! Every night she tries to pour me full of wine so she can sneak in and out. She's a lying bag of sneaky tricks. If I ever get inside, I'll fix you, wife.

(Anthony pushes Steffano and then hits him.)

ANTHONY: Stop! Shut your big mouth. You jack-ass. You idiot! You imbecile! Take that! My sister is much too good and pious for you.

STEFFANO: Anthony, let's talk this over. I'm not the fighting type.

GITTA: Hit him! Hit him again! Don't back away from him. He deserves it. You should hear the bad things he says about you brother.

STEFFANO: Stop! Brother-in-law, I plead with you. If you have a gripe with me, take me to court tomorrow.

ANTHONY: Ja! That is exactly what I'll do. Sister you come on home with me. Tomorrow we'll go to court. You come with me so this maniac doesn't try to hurt you. Come on sis, let's get out of here.

(They both exit and Steffano speaks.)

STEFFANO: Woe is me. Am I not the most miserable of men? I'm out-womanned by a crazy wife both in body and soul. I've suspected her for a long time, but she sure can out-trick me. I even end up being the guilty one. Pushed and slapped on top of that. Tomorrow they will haul me in before the judge and file the charges against me. My wife is the worst light that has ever been seen on earth. She can lie like a rug. I take the blame and end up begging her pardon. What should a poor dunce like me do? I guess I better just send two trustworthy gentleman over to see her in the morning. Maybe they can convince her to come home. I'll just have to put up with her devilish ways and tricks. Whenever she gets quarrelsome, I'll just give her whatever she wants. Maybe that will save me from more grief in my marriage — so says Hans Sachs.

The Farmer with the Blur

(1554)

A Carnival Play

Heinz Meier, the simple-minded farmer   Christa, Heinz's wife
Gretta, neighbor

(Heinz enters. He is carrying an axe.)

HEINZ: Ach! Shouldn't I complain about my bad luck? I get up before sunrise to come out here in the forest to chop wood. Once at the front door, I turn around a second to tell wife to bring me some soup as soon as possible. When I stuck my head in the window, I saw wife stark naked lying in bed with the priest. I felt like clobbering him. But I didn't because that priest is a shrewd one. He woulda threatened me with a ban. And I'd rather have beans than peas any day.[1] So I just walked away from the window madder than a penned-up goat. I called that priest a thief and a scoundrel and my wife a whore. I let fly a string of cuss words at both of them. Both of them there in bed heard what I thought. I'll get even on Sunday with the priest. When they pass the collection plate, he'll pay. And I'll yell at the top of my lungs, "The priest came into my house and laid my pious wife!" I'll cool his handle, and everyone will just stare at him.

When my wife brings me my soup today, I'll take care of her too. I'll tan her hide good with a thick stick. I'll break her in and ride her like a donkey—as they say. Right now I better get to work in the forest before the sun rises any more.

(The farmer exits. Christa enters scratching her head.)

CHRISTA: I'll be a pig's dead body! What should I do now? Husband was furious. The devil really baited me with that priest. The priest never gives me anything. He never bought me that pair of shoes. Not to mention the belt or shawl for the fair on New Year. He's the stingiest dog in the whole parish. And I am the biggest fool. He's so crude and clumsy with it. Besides his big mouth is as deformed as that hunch. That one-eyed rascal even stinks like a sheep. The devil really tricked me with that louse-filled father. No doubt the whole thing will be known by one and all. He not only takes my honor, which I never had much of, and then the whole matter becomes common gossip. Oh dear, I'm getting grey already from worry.

(The neighbor enters.)

GRETTA: Good morning, neighbor! Why are you tearing your hair, wailing and complaining? What's wrong with you?

CHRISTA: Oh dear neighbor, my husband woke up bright and early and went to chop wood in the forest. As soon as he was out the door, the priest snuck in and got in bed with me. My husband remembered he wanted to tell me something; so he came back and stuck his stupid head in the window. He saw the priest with me.

GRETTA: Oh neighbor! What did he do?

CHRISTA: Nothing. He walked away cussing a blue streak across the courtyard. I could see that murderous look in his eyes though. They ogled me like a fat hen, and then he called the priest a filthy rogue. Oh dear neighbor, what should I do? I'm really frightened to take my husband his soup. He will beat me blue. Advise me, what should I do?

GRETTA: You have a pious and simple-minded husband. But he's such a sheep. He won't punish you. Just make a clean slate of it. Then tell him, "Dear husband, forgive me for my shortcoming. It will never happen again." The whole affair will be over after you confess.

CHRISTA: Oh my husband has such heavy hands. Believe me I've felt them before. I know how he gets even. I don't trust him.

GRETTA: Dear neighbor, just stay home and bake your husband a cake. I'll go out in the forest and talk to your husband. I'm not afraid of him. He wouldn't hit me. I'll think of some trick to play on him. He is so simple-minded, he's as dumb as the Almighty's horse. I take that back. He's more ass than horse. I'll use my cunning wits to calm him down and make him forget his anger.

CHRISTA: If only he hadn't seen the priest, I could probably fool him

myself. But I fear all hope is lost, and I am going to pay dearly.
As they say, the heart is not deceived by what the eyes see. My
husband's suspicion is nothing to take lightly.

GRETTA: Dear neighbor, don't worry. I will uproot his suspicion and
cut out that anger as if somebody were pruning him with a knife.
I promise he'll even be begging your pardon that he carried on
so.

CHRISTA: Neighbor do help me. Help me to escape his beating and
scolding — and that priest gets off scot-free — and I swear I'll give
you a juicy ham in the bargain. Just get me out of trouble and
settle the thing happily.

GRETTA: No trouble. I'll fix everything. In the meantime, bake your
husband a cake. I'll arrange the whole thing just like your guardian
angel. Everything will be taken care of.

CHRISTA: Come on then. Let's bake him a cake full of eggs. And
don't spare any butter. Maybe with this crafty sweet, we can trick
his seeing-eyes. Maybe he'll forget his anger and his jealousy and
even his suspicion. Maybe it's true what they say — no mother of
invention lets her children be sad.

(They both exit. The farmer enters speaking to himself.)

HEINZ: Well, it must be almost noon. It's time for eating, if that
wicked wife of mine brings my soup! Here she comes now if I'm
not wrong. As soon as she puts my soup down, I'll grab her by
the hair and drag her back home. I'll get my club and tan her hide.
She'll be black, blue, and yellow when I get through punishing
her whoring ways with that priest. And on Sunday, I'll even the
score with him. He's goin' to wish three dollars he never came
in my house.

But look there! That woman isn't my wife. Am I losing my
wits or is that our neighbor bringing me my soup?

(Gretta enters.)

GRETTA: God greet you both this fine morning! Soup and fresh-baked
cake I'm bringing for both of you. Eat together and enjoy it.

(Heinz looks all around.)

HEINZ: Uh, neighbor, I'm alone.

GRETTA: I don't think so. I see you both. The two of you. Both of
you sit down quickly and eat before the soup gets cold.

(The farmer looks all around again.)

HEINZ: Neighbor, are you making fun of me?

GRETTA: My Heinz Meier, I am not making fun of you at all. I see you both — side by side. Now sit down together and eat your food. There's plenty for both of you.

(The farmer looks around and around.)

HEINZ: Gretta, I don't think you're very smart. Do you see two of me? I'm standing here all by myself. There's nobody else here with me.

GRETTA: Do you want me to swear an oath? You have black overalls on and so does he. I like that blue coat he has on. What do you mean there aren't two?

HEINZ: You better like it because I'm standing here. Grab the other wherever he is.

(Gretta grabs in the air.)

GRETTA: Pig dirt! You're right Heinz. Nothing there. Now I know what's wrong. I've got the blur. But I sure would have bet my body and soul that I saw two of you. In fact, I still see more of you.

HEINZ: What is this blur, neighbor?

GRETTA: Why Heinz, whoever gets up before sun-up and goes out before daybreak has fog and mist in their eyes. You just can't see clear. Often you see plain double.

HEINZ: So you mean I had the blur this morning in my eyes? You mean the blur made me think the priest was lying in bed with my wife? It made me scorn and curse them both?

GRETTA: Absolutely. The blur deceived you and made you bleary-eyed and suspicious. You got up too early. Oh it happens to me too. A lot. Early mornings I look at our cow and see two. And our dog. And other things too. Whenever I get up early to go to church, I often see two of them as well.

HEINZ: What rotten luck I got the blur. I was so bleary-eyed I coulda sworn I saw two lumps on that priest's back. And that would have been real bad luck if I had pounded and beat up on them.

GRETTA: You must forget the insults that you shamefully made. You should beg the forgiveness of your pious wife and priest.

HEINZ: Yes, I'll do it. I'll even give the priest an extra penny on Sunday just because I was so suspicious of him. And I won't yell at my wife anymore. In fact, I'll buy her the new red purse that she wants — just as sure as I thought I saw that tonsure as clear as

a plate. But thanks to you neighbor I understand the whole thing.
People are sure fooled by that blur. But you've set me straight on
this thing. I mean what my eyes see is without a doubt true.[2]

GRETTA: That's right dear Heinz. More or less. Just remember — you
can't beat the blur. So sleep late long after sun-up and you won't
get the night-mist blurring your eyes. Otherwise you'll see a goat
and think it's a gardner and go running off full of jealousy and
fury.

HEINZ: Come on Gretta, let's go home to my wife. Help me beg
forgiveness for my insults to her and also that pious priest. I'll
apologize to him too. We can all sit down in the tavern and forget
all this ill-humor. Bring on the wine, and I'll bring out my wursts.
We'll push all these sad events away. Let's forget the blurs and
brouhahas — so wishes Hans Sachs in Nuremburg.

The Evil Woman

(1553)

A Carnival Play

Bachelor

Else, a maid

Neighbor

The Evil Woman

The Evil Woman's husband

(The Bachelor enters and speaks.)

BACHELOR: Greetings, ladies and gentlemen. It's my pleasant task to come here this evening to present to you a subject concerning good manners and honor. Now, I know, it goes without saying, that everybody here is honorable and up-standing. I confess that I wanted to have a good time tonight. So I teased or should I say "won" seven coins[1] from a stableboy over at the market place. I want to spend them all on you right now. Being completely virtuous, showing good manners and honor, let's while away the time playing skittles, drinking, and carousing. At least until the evening bell rings. Bring on the bottles and pour yourselves a drink. Let's all be happy and be of good cheer!

(The Maid enters with a mug.
She looks all around and then speaks.)

ELSE: Good evening! Excuse me. Where is the wine cellar? I'm s'posed to fetch some muscatel. Am I in the right place? Did my master come in this evening with his neighbor?

(The Bachelor walks up to the Maid and speaks very friendly to her.)

BACHELOR: Ja! You are completely right. They both were right there drinking. Dear Else, how long it has been since I've had a chance to talk to you. Things have been going so well for us and we're so busy. There's never any time in the master's house for me to tell you any of my secrets. I wish I could open my heart to you.

(The Maid answers mockingly.)

ELSE: I see this is your idea of a joke.

BACHELOR: No, I'm serious. Honest.

ELSE: "Open your heart"? Then go get a can-opener.

BACHELOR: My heart is sinking in love for you.

ELSE: Well, don't let it drown! Better yet go let two pigs blow on it.

BACHELOR: Must my honor be scorned like this? My heart is over-
come with grief and pain.

ELSE: Maybe it's heartburn, huh? Did you have a peacock for supper?

BACHELOR: Ach! No, my heart is so wounded by you.

ELSE: Then go to the hospital if you're so unhealthy.

BACHELOR: Oh miss, don't deny me! With your goodness you can
comfort me. Otherwise I shall have no hope.

ELSE: If I had a sheepskin with cold water, I'd revive you fast enough.

BACHELOR: Oh with your soul-felt sight make my longing heart well.

ELSE: I don't have any time now. Why don't you just sit down and
wait awhile. Or come back tomorrow so you can hang a door for
me.

BACHELOR: Oh how you want to make my heart sick! Won't you
enjoy my faithfulness and true love? Oh, unlock your heart to
me.

ELSE: Too bad. I lost the key.

BACHELOR: I have never had eyes for anyone but you. Above all, you
are the one who pleases me the most.

ELSE: You have it easy. Go please yourself.

BACHELOR: Oh, to you alone would I give myself. My honor and
property, life and limb in order to pay homage to none but you.

ELSE: I don't want any of those things!

BACHELOR: Oh, these harsh words. Things could become boring after
awhile.

ELSE: Well, then I'll call the piper so that he can play an ape dance
for you.

BACHELOR: If you'll make me a crown, I'll dance happily for you.

ELSE: Everything silly makes a child happy. Besides, I've never
crowned an ass.

BACHELOR: You're taunting me now with scorn. Stop your abuse and
disdain, and show me some pity.

ELSE: Don't you know? Hoping and waiting only make fools. And
you'll sit a long time waiting for me.

BACHELOR: Can't you see, I'm sweating from so much longing? Grant me some small grace.

ELSE: You are sweating in a fool's tub. I'm not the Pope in Rome. Neither grace nor indulgence will you ever get from me.

BACHELOR: Just let me be yours!

ELSE: I repeat, "no"!

BACHELOR: You're robbing me of all joy. How long will you hold out?

ELSE: You can do just as you please. I didn't ask you to come here. You can come and go whenever you wish.

BACHELOR: I know you can't leave me.

ELSE: Ach! Then you leave me. Go on your way. You have all my permission and power.

BACHELOR: Oh my poor heart is breaking. My exciting, beautiful Else you are harder than a rock. Let my friendly requests soften you!

ELSE: No, you'll not fleece any sheep here. Don't come prattling on my ears with courting words. I can see you're a rogue, and I'm not falling for your tricks. You'd leave me high and dry like many a poor maid.

BACHELOR: Oh dear. My love. No, on my oath, I wouldn't. I want to marry you.

ELSE: Oh really? If that were true, you'd be pledging and promising a lot more.

BACHELOR: Darling Else, trust me! I'm saying it with all sincerity and goodness.

ELSE: Oh sure! I heard all this recently. The horse of sincerity just rode right over me. I was the butt of the joke, and now I don't trust so easily. Oh my God! Run! Run! My mistress is coming.

(The Evil Woman enters. She looks around maliciously.)

EVIL WOMAN: So! Here you stand half the night oogling. Move it, you little dirt bag. Go take the chair and sit down next to him! You'll never stand again. Supper time for Miss Chatterbox! You're more deceitful than the mayor. For such an errand you could have gone to death and back! You were supposed to come right home. Did you hear me?

ELSE: I don't exactly have wings. How quick do you want?

EVIL WOMAN: Ach! Somebody will give them to you after one ride on you. Why are you just standing there?

ELSE: You have to wait for the wine.

EVIL WOMAN: You still have a lot of wash to do. You've got the itch from dawn to dusk! You won't be happy 'til you're pregnant. Then, you'll go boasting around. Well, I won't take care of you or your bastard kid.

BACHELOR: Madam, we were standing here in complete innocence just talking! Be considerate and leave!

(*The Evil Woman shouts at the Bachelor.*)

EVIL WOMAN: You blockhead! It's none of your business. Leave us and go back to work. You couldn't pay a tailor for thread because you haven't worked a Monday yet. You're as lazy as she is. I'll rout you out of here.

BACHELOR: Madam. Mind your own business! My master pays me a salary. Besides, I want nothing to do with a streetwalker like you.

EVIL WOMAN: Ha! Look at you! You and your syphilitic scabs! You'll eat those words you drunken buffoon!

BACHELOR: You deny them yourself, you yellow cyst. You've tried out almost every farm laborer around.

EVIL WOMAN: Leave me alone you idiot, or I'll call the Master.

ELSE: M'am even if you do, it won't help any.

(*The Evil Woman turns to the Maid.*)

EVIL WOMAN: Quiet, you scamp! Are you still standing there? Move! You dirt bag! You hustler!

ELSE: Maybe you're referring to yourself? Who is the bag and who hustles?

EVIL WOMAN: Out now or I'll knock your teeth down your throat!

(*The Bachelor gets between them.*)

BACHELOR: Lady, then you'll never chew again either. Go Else. Go and complain to the clergyman.

EVIL WOMAN: What business is this of yours? You womanizer. You play-boy. You gallow-gland.

(*Evil Woman turns to the Maid.*)

EVIL WOMAN: And you, filth face, give me back my key. You're fired!

(*The Maid returns the key and says.*)

ELSE: There! Now pay me my wages.

EVIL WOMAN: What?

ELSE: Just that. You owe me for six months.

EVIL WOMAN: My dear trollop is that right? Well, what about the plates you've broken and your garbage cooking? You owe me.!

ELSE: You lie like a rug.

EVIL WOMAN: You through your teeth.

ELSE: You cheat.

(The Husband rushes on stage.)

HUSBAND: What in the hell is going on here? Screaming like the devil
  is dancing. I was just passing by, and I thought it was a mob riot
  in here. Why are you all screaming? It sounds like a wolf hunt.
  Shame on you, before all of these up-standing people. Are you
  crazy? In God's name go home. It's high-time.

(The Evil Woman goes crying to her husband.)

EVIL WOMAN: Oh dear husband. Just look. Your maid and this hired-
  hand have insulted and shamed me. All these people are my
  witness. Why don't you ask what they've done to me?

BACHELOR: Sir, let me explain! Your wife attacked both of us and our
  honor. We retaliated in the same fashion, and we were defending
  ourselves when you came in.

(The Husband blesses himself.)

HUSBAND: Ach, woe is me. You shouldn't carry on so. Else, you
  have plenty of work to keep busy. And, Alta, you are too quick
  to anger. Let's just sit down and enjoy some wine and put an end
  to all of this.

(The wife shouts.)

EVIL WOMAN: Throw that hussy out of the house! I never want to see
  her again. She tried to shame our marriage. She's a liar and a
  wastrel. She's lazy as manure and steals on the sly.

(The Maid throws up both hands and speaks.)

ELSE: You lie through your gums. I was always a good servant. I've
  put up with your fits, manias, lies, and shams. I never want to
  hear you howl again or put up with your treachery. I quit!

(The woman screams.)

EVIL WOMAN: You wash-bowl mouth! Tell us more. Tell the master!

ELSE: Sure, I'll spill some more that will really open his eyes.

(The woman slaps her hands together and gnashes her teeth.)

EVIL WOMAN: I'll rip you apart! Now you've run-off. I never did
  such a thing.

ELSE: We're like water buckets on a pole. We both hang together.
    You better believe it.

EVIL WOMAN: You public box! Who will give me your hide?

ELSE: Try yourself.

EVIL WOMAN: Do you dare?

ELSE: You know and I know. Should I spell it out—loud and clear?

(The Evil Woman jumps on the maid.)

EVIL WOMAN: I'll plug that evil hole of yours. Let's have at it.

(The Husband stands between them and speaks.)

HUSBAND: Shame on you both for doing this here! But the dog sure
    did bark a lot this year before dawn. So you both were in cahoots?
    I couldn't understand it, but now I'm beginning to see the light
    too. You're both alike as far as honor is concerned. Real pure
    and right—like my left shoe.

(The woman screams.)

EVIL WOMAN: What? And just who do you bed? Ha! Ha! Ha! It's
    true. I've suspected you for the whole year too. You like your
    maid, don't you?

HUSBAND: Shut up! Or I'll beat you.

EVIL WOMAN: You want to hit me on her account, right? I'll go to my
    friend then. That'll cost you. You scoundrel, you are her lover!
    I found your handkerchief under her straw mattress. You villain.
    You betrayer. Sneak, I wish you were at the bottom of the Necker
    River with your whore. Gallow-balls!

(The Husband snatches the key from his wife's hand.)

HUSBAND: Give me my key! Leave! I'm ashamed of you.

EVIL WOMAN: What? You want to take my house key? You want
    to throw me out? No. That will not be. You are the cheat that
    wrecked my marriage. You drink yourself stupid and then pass
    out in bed. I'm going to the judge.

(The Husband shakes his fist.)

HUSBAND: And I'm going to push your mouth in.

EVIL WOMAN: Who? Mine?

HUSBAND: Yes. Yours.

EVIL WOMAN: The devil protect you if you try.

(The Husband raises his arm.)

HUSBAND: Shut up! Or I'll smash your ear.

EVIL WOMAN: Who? Mine?

HUSBAND: Yes. Yours.

(The Evil Woman gives him the finger.)

EVIL WOMAN: Do it! Today's as good as tomorrow.

HUSBAND: I won't spare you. I'll beat that evil right out of you.

EVIL WOMAN: Do it. I'm not going to stand around all day. You've already killed seven men so why not increase the number? Don't worry about a trace, you can cover everything up.

(Husband hits her.)

HUSBAND: Shut up! Shut up, you hussy! Or I'll beat you to a cripple.

(The woman screams.)

EVIL WOMAN: I hear you! You gross idiot! Help me! Someone help me! Murder!

(The Neighbor opens the door and runs in.)

NEIGHBOR: What's going on here? I thought the whole house was burning. You scared me to death and awakened my child. What a mess! Tell me neighbor, what is the meaning of all this? Why are you so furious? And all of your servants here?

(The wife approaches, crying.)

EVIL WOMAN: Oh, my dear neighbor. Just look. All three of them — my husband, my maid, the servant — all of them shamed me. They all ganged-up against me.

HUSBAND: Dear neighbor, we are the three who have been insulted and abused by her rantings and ravings. I can't tell you how bad it is. Now she screams bloody murder as if we have done her the harm.

NEIGHBOR: Dear madam, I suspect the guilt is yours not theirs. We see you frothing at someone everyday. You're violent and should be put away. Or for God's sake change your ways, and give us some peace.

EVIL WOMAN: What devil blew you in here! You gossiping, brawling, bowlegged chatterbox. I don't need your two cents worth. You're a snake slithering from one corner to the next. You gorge and booze with my husband and let me starve at home. You gamble away your money and then come after ours. You chase after anything that walks or limps if she looks at you. Both of you should be run out of town.

HUSBAND: Just look, my neighbor. Now you know that my wife
    has no honor. Every day she's like that. Her whining, nagging,
    complaining has taken the final toll. I can't take it any longer.
    I'm worn out. If I took religious vows I'd be happier.

NEIGHBOR: I've noticed for a long time that you are the fool in your
    own house. But you're not alone. I can name plenty of others just
    like you. They're all afraid of their wives, and they can't move
    an inch one way or the other.

EVIL WOMAN: Ha! You should laugh! You're as big a fool as he is.
    Your wife rules in your house with her club. You're the biggest
    fool in the parish. Ha! And you try and blame me?

BACHELOR: Ach! Quit your babbling! You sound like an old hen
    crowing. Look at her, she's whistling over the ruins. She's put
    us all in the dirt.

EVIL WOMAN: Yeah. And you think like a silly goose. You walk
    around like a little boy not yet shaving.

ELSE: And you lock me in the bread closet and read me the Psalms
    as if I had burned the whole town. I'm glad this is ending. You
    can't stand to see somebody else dance.

EVIL WOMAN: Shut up! You worthless, lousy flea-bag. You sneak
    thief. I'll fix you all — neighbor, maid, servant, and you, you
    unconscious dope. Go scratch your head. You'll end up in court
    and I'll fleece your hide. The hang-man will crow over you.

NEIGHBOR: My God. Stop your wife. Look how her eyes spark and
    her face is on fire! Look how she gnashes her teeth and her hands
    shake and her feet stamp. She looks like an ass in spasm. I'm
    afraid she's gone beserk. Mad. Insane. Let's lock her up!

HUSBAND: Look at her. She's got St. Urban's plague. That's why
    she carries on so all day long. That's why you can hear her clear
    over at your house. Look at her evil!

NEIGHBOR: So show your manly courage, or she'll ride you forever.
    She'll be master of your house and all will be ashamed of you.
    Grab a club and blast her between the ears.

EVIL WOMAN: You louse! You're the devil. You set my husband
    against me? I'll take all four of you in a fight.

NEIGHBOR: Don't let her scorn us. Save mankind or she will eat us
    alive. Slam her with the chair. Hit her! Hit her! Crack her nut!

*(All five fight over the chair. The Evil
Woman pulls it away and swings wildly.)*

EVIL WOMAN: Ah-hah! I've got it. Here, here, and there! Take that you wicked squirts. I'll show you how to bash. I'll drive you out of here!

(*Everybody runs out the door. The Bachelor returns and speaks.*)

BACHELOR: My dear ladies and gentlemen. It is my request and hope that you won't be angry with me since this fight began. I came in here tonight in peace and good humor. And then that virago came in and threw everybody out. I'll take the shame for all of us and hope for the best. You all know, without doubt, that women want to be masters! It's so deep rooted in them here, there, and everywhere. But the new lesson tells us that the time for a turn-about is now. Me? I'm staying single so that I'm not wo-manned. I'll carry my own lamp so that I'm not beaten and bruised out of my own house. Thereby, I'll be spared from shame and unhappiness. God protect you all forever and ever.[2]

The Grand Inquisitor in the Soup

(1553)

A Carnival Play

Simon, the simple-minded innkeeper   Herman Pich, informer
Clas, Simon's neighbor   Sexton
Inquisitor

(Herman Pich enters.)

HERMAN: What can I do to improve things? For some time now I've
been walking around looking for a customer who might fill my
pockets. They sure are empty. Wait. Here comes simple Simon.
He's as rich in gold and goods as he is poor in common sense
and courage. I have tricked him many times and many places —
especially in his own tavern. I wonder where he's going so early
in the morning? I'll greet him and find out. "Hello. Where to so
early? When do we want to go drinking?"

(Simon enters.)

SIMON: I'm on my way to town to get some oats, hay, and straw
for my guests' animals. But let me also tell you I just got the
best Alsatian wine! I'll bet even God or John the Baptist — or
whoever it was — I can't ever remember — would say this wine is
tremendous. It'll bring pleasure to all. I know you wouldn't cuss
it either. Come on over this afternoon and try it. Bring a friend
or two with you.

HERMAN: Ja! Of course we'll come. Too bad we couldn't have a
fresh fowl or two along with a game of chess, dice, and cards.

SIMON: I'll be waiting for you without fail. But right now I must be
on my way. I'll be back home around noon.

(Simon exits. Herman speaks to himself.)

HERMAN: Oh indeed I'll come see you. But for the moment, you've given me the word I wanted to hear. Ha! You idiot, it will cost you dear as soon as the Inquisitor hears. That fat old monk will teach you some *morae*. I'm off to the monastery right now to see him. And hopefully, there will be a payback for me.

(*Herman exits. Doctor Romanus, the Inquisitor, enters.*)

INQUISITOR: Doctor Romanus, the Inquisitor, is my name. I've been sent here by Rome to suppress any heresy that I find — in word or deed, here or in other places — by young or old, by rich or by poor. I hold Papal authority to penalize and levy fines, to sanction or to strangle or to burn, to throw fear into the commoner, that is my mission. At the same time, by tricks and intrigues, any money, gifts, or goodies are all most welcome in my purse.[1]

Actually my position hasn't brought me that much. My cow is about all I've gotten so far. Nevertheless, I've got some good customers in this town and elsewhere. Whenever my informers hear a word that blasphemes the Holy See or if someone takes God's name in vain, they whisper it in my ear. Then I howl "heresy" and make them kneel, as I look for their purse. I squeeze 'til the guilders ease out. Why not? These fools don't know any differently. Afterwards I dispense a little grace. Wait — here comes Herman Pich. He's brought me lots of heretics. Let's see what this is about. Over here! Herman Pich, what brings you here?

(*Herman enters and bows.*)

HERMAN: Doctor, I bring good news. I've caught a fat bird.
INQUISITOR: Tell me, what has he done?
HERMAN: Do you know Simon, the rich innkeeper? He's the one I've stalked.
INQUISITOR: I don't know him. What has he done?
HERMAN: Today when I was taking a walk I met Simon walking along as merrily as could be. He cheerfully told me he had the best of wines. He bragged it was so wonderful — and in a very scornful tone — even if St. John or even God drank some of it they'd sink under the table and be drunk as pigs.
INQUISITOR: Ah-hah! That's heresy if ever! I'll get him *per Deum* before he gets away. I'll comb his purse for sure. Tell me, is he rich?
HERMAN: Oh indeed. Nobody in town is as rich. His wealth overflows like his wonderful wine stock and supply. On the other hand, he is

simple-minded, somewhat coarse, and dumb like a peasant. He's a good one to pluck.

INQUISITOR: Yes indeed. I'll clip his wings with utmost care. You shall have a part in the plot as well. Tell me, do you know where he lives?

HERMAN: His house is over on Long Street.

INQUISITOR: Excellent. I'll send my porter over there immediately to summon him. Then I shall squeeze him until he himself denies God.

(They both exit. Simon enters moaning.)

SIMON: Oh no! Oh! Ahhh! Ach! Oh I'm in great danger now. I'll be a pig's dead body! I'm so afraid. Woe is me. What can I do?

(Clas, Simon's neighbor, enters.)

CLAS: Simon, why in heaven's name are you groaning so? What's wrong with you? Why such whimpering and complaining?

SIMON: Ach, dear neighbor, I am complaining with every good reason. The Nequamsitter sent his partner to fetch me to the monastery.

CLAS: You mean the Inquisitor sent his porter to summon you?

SIMON: I mean our town's 'vestigator of hairsey.[2] That stingy, fat, larded, monk—who else do you think I'm talking about?

CLAS: Ah yes. None other. It's the same old story. You must have said something that sounded irreverent. Now he wants to say you're a heretic.

SIMON: Oh no! God must have done something. I don't know of anything I did. Honest. That monk is so arrogrunt. And he really punishes and shames people. He's been so strict for years on folks. How come he wants to drag me along? Oh, I know he'll get me all tangled up in my words. Oh dear neighbor. Clas, please go with me. If you go, I'll give you a whole litre of that new wonderful Alsatian wine. Help me defend myself against that mean old monk.

CLAS: You haven't insulted anyone, and you didn't eat any meat on Friday, so just calm yourself. The monk is not going to eat you alive.

SIMON: But I can't answer all his questions. I'm too simple-minded for that monk. He confuses me with all his words. Neighbor Clas, won't you go with me?

CLAS: Of course, I will. I'll go right now with you to the convent of the bare-claws. He asked you to come so indeed we will. He'll probably ask you a few questions and then ask you for a horse or wagon. Presto! Honor restored.

SIMON: Go on. I'll gladly give him that. But we better leave 'cuz it's after three o'clock and that's when they go to choir. Oh my hair is standing on end.

(Both exit. The Inquisitor and the Sexton enter.)

INQUISITOR: Sexton, go and light the candles. It's time for service. Be sure and tell the brothers to sing devoutly so all the people think we're holy, pious, and spiritual. That way everybody — young and old — will bring us their offerings. Ha! Then we'll make a soup your body won't soon forget. What's left over we'll give to the poor at noontime when they line up outside the cloister. Make a kettle for them and mix in some herbs, peas, and radishes. That's enough for them. Like the old proverb says, "If the poor have a lot — then they eat a lot."

SEXTON: Worthy Father, don't you worry about a thing. I'll do exactly as you wish. That soup is only good for beggars. Obviously, we'll remove any meat or pieces of fish and save these for ourselves for our own meal this afternoon. In any event, the commoners will continue thinking that we give the poor our own food and that we live frugally and in extreme moderation. They will continue to believe we subsist on soup or porridge and then fast the rest of the day. Let them think this. So much the better. Then they'll bring us even more offerings.

   Is that Simon who is coming here? And the other man? What do they want?

INQUISITOR: I plan to examine that bumpkin with the sharpest and most confusing words he has ever heard. He let a word slip, and I've got him by his ears. I'll separate a few dollars from him. Ha. He'll pay for some of our meals and his repentance may even bring us some delightful fish. Go on now and tell the brothers to start singing the *Gaudiamus* and to play the organ loudly. We'll get something out of this.

(The Sexton exits. Simon enters.)

SIMON: Holy Father, God be with you! I'm here as you commanded.
INQUISITOR: Are you Simon the innkeeper whom I have summoned?
SIMON: Yessir, Holy Father.
INQUISITOR: Oh! You poisonous, murderous blasphemer. Can't even God in heaven be spared from your heretical tongue? And St.

John the Baptist as well? Do you dare make of him a wine bibber who drinks two kegs of wine? You, you drunkard and all of those just like you! Such opinions are pure heresy. You deserve nothing short of fire in hell like all monstrous heretics. And so it will be. Your poor soul will burn forever when you die. Eternal burning.

CLAS: Simon, think a minute. Did you say such things about God?

SIMON: Well, this morning I did see Herman Pich, and I told him I had a wonderful new Alsatian wine. I said that if even God or St. John alone had some of this wine they would think it timely and good. It would gladden their hearts and make them happy. That's what I said and nothing more.

CLAS: Mercy me, that's not a bit harmful, you just repeated an old proverb. That wouldn't shame God at all. Don't worry, you are not going to lose body and soul over this. Sir, temper your anger and let the good man go back home. Don't make a mountain out of a mole hill.

INQUISITOR: Huh! What do you know about these things? Why are you even with a heretic? Do you know what a heretic is?

CLAS: Sir, I've known for quite a while. Someone who pulls ticks out of his hair!

INQUISITOR: I don't appreciate your derision.

CLAS: Sir, I'm not sticking my tongue out at anybody. But you talk like a slate — smooth and hard.

INQUISITOR: Why you're an advocate of this heretic. I shall place you in an excommunicatory ban.

CLAS: If I can't eat beans, I'll go to peas.[3]

INQUISITOR: My word, I think you're possessed. Remember you are on holy ground. If you continue uttering such foolish words, I shall eject you from my parish!

CLAS: Dear Sir, I think you are the fool. You are the one who is making all the ruckus and rumpus. And you've got something up your sleeve, don't you? By my word too, I think you have a dunce cap around your neck.

INQUISITOR: You jack-ass! Go blow your nose elsewhere! I want nothing more to do with you.

CLAS: You yourself are the gross ass; and you think you can run around making propaganda just because you wear a cowl and collar.

INQUISITOR: Get out! Get out of this monastery! Leave me, you bag of dirt. You vomiting bird of iniquity.

CLAS: You're the dirty bird, although you smell more like a goat.

And you've pulled the wool over people's eyes too long. So don't blame me dear sir, even if I have had a few good drinks. Just try and show a little piety until I return.

(The neighbor exits.)

INQUISITOR: Who is that scoundrel who spoke so shamefully to me? I shall not tolerate him a moment longer. In fact, it is my full intention to bring his name to the papal authorities. Tell me! Isn't his name Schmidt?

SIMON: Holy Father, I don't know him. He acts like he's drunk. Crazy or completely boozed. He seemed alright when he came in with me.

INQUISITOR: He'll find no dummy in me. Now, what should I do with you? You are an heretic and under the threat of papal ban. You should be thrown to the fire.

SIMON: Oh! Pardon me, worthy father. Spare me my life. Doesn't God forgive us our sins when we ask for mercy and forgiveness with all one's heart?

INQUISITOR: Your sins weigh heavily against you. You will remain here in the monastery. In the meantime, I shall write to the Pope in Rome about your heresy and immoral slander against God. Perhaps, as penance, you will have to go to Rome on a pilgrimage with other fallen souls. Or drink the waters of the Tiber or visit the holy land in order to erase your scandalous mutterings against God. But for now, go in the chapel and listen to my sermon and meet me here afterwards. Then you will repeat to me what you have learned. And don't think I'll go easy on you for having done this penance. Only I can absolve you. I'm going to give the sermon, follow me immediately.

(The Inquisitor exits. Clas re-enters.)

CLAS: My dear neighbor. Tell me! How are you doing here in the monastery? Are you afraid?

SIMON: And how! Now that I'm entangled in this monastery-mess they've threatened to send me to Rome to stand before the Pope. Or to burn me or maybe even drown me!

CLAS: Don't even think about it, neighbor. That stingy monk doesn't want your blood. He wants your money and property. Give him three dozen dollars to pay for your heresy. Then see how fast you'll be out of here.

SIMON: Oh! I would gladly give a hundred dollars cash just to escape the fire. I never thought that my money could free me. I shoulda thought of that long ago. I figured the best way was to plea, beg, and fast my way out. But now, I have to go into the chapel to hear the sermon. I'm supposed to report to the monk after his sermon.

CLAS: Listen to me. Just follow my advice. What's to lose? You'll be out in no time.

SIMON: I'd really like to, believe me. Everybody preaches how bad purgatory is, but it couldn't be nearly as monstrous as this place.

CLAS: Well, come on, I'll go with you to the chapel. Let's go hear what the monk says about victims and sinners.

(They both exit. The Inquisitor and Sexton enter.)

SEXTON: Tell me worthy Father, highest benefactor of our convent. How does the matter stand with Simon, the innkeeper? Did you examine him? Has the cow given any milk?

INQUISITOR: He acts exactly the same. It's as if he didn't understand. In fact, he begged me to forgive his sins, and he even quoted Holy Scripture to me! The whole time he didn't even mention money or goods. I'll tighten the ropes a little more, and he'll cry and blubber. But he'll come to see that the way out is with money. There comes the oaf from my sermon now.

(Simon enters.)

INQUISITOR: You, heretic! You heard the sermon? What did you learn?

SIMON: Holy Father. I heard the most horrible news. I am troubled beyond belief.

INQUISITOR: What is it? Do you doubt what you heard? Speak up, man. I will instruct you.

SIMON: Oh Sir. I don't doubt it one bit. I'm not worried at all for me.

INQUISITOR: Speak up! What did the sermon teach?

SIMON: You said in the sermon "that what you give here on earth will be returned a hundred times in heaven."

INQUISITOR: That is true. Therefore, if you give a lot to the monastery, you will be repaid a hundred fold. What frightens you about this teaching?

SIMON: For me, I'm not at all worried. But I sure am afraid for you and the whole convent.

INQUISITOR: Why for us? Speak up!

SIMON: Well, I've seen how everyday you give three big kettles of
soup to the poor. And you do that day in and day out the whole
year. So that's three times three hundred and sixty-five or one
thousand ninety-five kettles a year. Then you multiply that by
one hundred kettles full that you'll get up there. Whew! What
will you do with all that soup? Truly, I fear the whole convent
will sink and drown. Whoever can't swim — with your wide cowls
and robes — will be pulled to the bottom. You'll be buried in soup!
Oh poor you! What suffering for all of you.

INQUISITOR: Ach! You toad! Damn you! You heretic! You, you
scoundrel. You dunce! How dare you! Who perverted you so?
You're under papal excommunication for life! Scorn us, will you?
Leave the monastery at once. Go to the gallows in your own
house. Don't ever appear before me again! Be gone!

SIMON: Sir, you don't have to forbid me not to come back. I'd rather
have stayed home in the first place. I must say that I have not seen
much goodness here in the cloister. I've seen hypocrisy, lots of
mumbling words, but very little devotion. You put quite a show
on for the world — but it's all a very bad scene. Ach! I leave
knowing now.

(Simon exits and the Inquisitor closes.)

INQUISITOR: Look at that! Just look, sexton. He's crazy, hardened,
cursed. The common man no longer fears us or our threat of
ban. Although we've squeezed them for a lot, they're beginning
to see our game. Our deception is leaking out. They don't trust
us anymore and are going to the Bible. The beam in our house
is starting to weaken and our foundation of bishops and cardinals
is starting to stagger. In fact, it's already starting to fall — so says
Hans Sachs.

The Dead Man

(1554)

A Carnival Play

Hans, the husband   The Neighbor
Wife   The Neighbor's wife

(*The Husband and Wife enter.*)

WIFE: Oh dear husband, Hans. There's something I want to ask you. Please say you won't say "no". Please tell me how much you really love me. I really want to know.

HANS: I can't grant you that wish. You seem to act in two different ways. Sometimes I love you, and sometimes I don't so much. I really can't answer you.

WIFE: Well, dear Hans, tell me then why you love me, when you do love me. Then I'll know.

HANS: Well, when you do everything I tell you to, loyally, obediently and willingly — then I love you. I share everything with you. I see to it that you have all the clothes, jewelry, food and drink you need. Whatever I do, I do it just to please you. And if you do likewise, one love for another, we'd both love each other. Our love would then grow each day.

WIFE: Well, dear Hans, tell me now why is it sometimes you don't love me? Tell me so I can guard against it, so you'll always love me.

HANS: Alright. I'll tell you. When you go against my will, publicly or in secret, then it comes over me, and I don't love you. Do you understand?

WIFE: Oh dearest husband, what do I do that displeases you?

HANS: · Oh, countless things everyday you do just by your words or actions. It makes me suffer a lot.

WIFE: Dear husband, tell me. What?

HANS: Why can't you tell yourself? You know you're lazy when it comes to housekeeping. You think I'm lax and call me lazy. You're sometimes angry and malicious and you seldom ever defend me. You always want to be right, as if I were the wife and you the husband. See, so your great thoughtlessness and bad behavior works on me. And you just break my love to pieces.

WIFE: Well, dear husband, if you let such things worry you, your love for me is weak to start with. If you loved me as I love you, your love wouldn't go to pieces that easily. It would grow strong and more solid every day.

HANS: Wife, while we're talking about it, I'd just like to know. Have you ever loved me in all these days?

WIFE: Me? But husband, why shouldn't I? Don't you know I do? All the time I call you "dearest Hans" don't you see my love always?

HANS: But that is just words. I never saw it in your actions. In fact, I see just the opposite and about everyday too!

WIFE: Now dear husband, I'll show you my true love. I've loved you so much all these years; if you were ill, I'd gladly die for you. And if you'd die before me, I wouldn't want to live on alone without you. I wouldn't want another husband either. Honest. I'd have them bury you in my coat, the one that's rosy-red, like the lilac bush I love. Then everyone would have to say they'd never seen a greater love. By my faith, I swear it.

HANS: If your love endures and lasts like this, as you say, then it's greater than wine. I plan to start enjoying your love right now.

WIFE: Yes, dear. Such is my love. Believe me. Honest. I never told you before because I was afraid you'd take me for granted. But right now, I'll even go down to the Pegnits River and do our wash. You stay home, all right?

HANS: You go and wash. I'll stay home and kill time by the stove. I'll check over the apples and pears here. I'll just eat the small ones.

(Wife exits. Hans speaks to himself.)

HANS: Well, well. My wife prides herself on her great love. I sure never felt much though. She'll probably only show her love after I'm gone, dead and buried. I'd enjoy it more if she showed her love while I'm still alive. I would live better, wouldn't I? When I'm dead, what good does it do for her crying and carrying-on?

Still, I'd like to know what she really thinks. Hmm. I think
I'll just find out. I'll just lie down right here, stretch out — full
length — as if I just died. I'll try and hold my breath. When she
comes back, she'll think I'm dead. Then I'll see for sure what
pain and crying there is for my death. I'll see just how beautifully
she'd have me buried in the red coat just like she promised. By
Jove, I'll try it! I'll play dead as a doornail.

(Hans stretches out on the floor. Wife
returns from doing her wash.)

WIFE: Look at the fool! Stretched out on the floor like a lazy groom.
Hans! Hans, what are you doing? Get up! Help me hang up the
wash.

(Wife looks at him closely. Shakes him.)

WIFE: Come on now, dear Hans. Get up. You aren't dead are you?
Yes! Yes, I see it now, he's dead all right! What should I do?
Should I cry or eat first? If I start crying and moaning, all the
neighbors will come running. Then I'd have to cry even more, a
lot more. I wouldn't get a thing to eat all night. And look — I'm
wet all over from the wash — I'll put on dry clothes first. Then
I'll fry some eggs in lard, so to be able to cry and lament. I'll
go down to the cellar too, get me a quart of wine to drink, just to
refresh myself, in my grief. Like the old proverb says: "To dance
and cry on an empty stomach has never done anyone any good."

(Wife exits singing. Hans sits up and speaks.)

HANS: Ho! Ho! That love is cold as ice. She did herself proud. My
death grieves her as much as dropping a spoon. Good Lord — who
is that knocking now?

(Neighbor's Wife enters. Wife re-enters.)

WIFE: Neighbor look! Just look here! I went to do wash and while
I was away, my husband went and died on me. I'm ruined! He
kept me well all my life. Just lately, I did learn to love him. Oh
what pain! What grief!

NEIGHBOR'S WIFE: He's dead, you say? Why he was a good man,
your husband. Never would harm a fly. By my faith, he was a
good neighbor! Sure sorry to see him go. Tell me, neighbor, what
ailed him?

WIFE: He stuck himself in the finger yesterday. He's always been a
puny fellow. Cost me a pretty penny, he did. I never skimped on

anything for him, no matter how much it cost. To make a long
story short—I just spent five dollars on herbs and spices for his
steam bath yesterday.

NEIGHBOR'S WIFE: It's a sorry thing that he's dead. But it can't be
changed. You'll just have to accept it. God does all things in
time!

WIFE: That's easy for you to say. It's me who has no more husband.
Who'll support me now?

NEIGHBOR'S WIFE: Go get yourself a new husband. He'll be just like
this last one, our neighbor here. He'll support you.

WIFE: But, I can't! Tomorrow is Fastnacht, Lenten season. Those
priests have fixed it so nobody can celebrate a wedding during
carnival time. Oh neighbor, what oh what am I to do? I never
thought keeping house was so hard without a husband.

NEIGHBOR'S WIFE: You'll just have to shake off your grief. Go get
your red coat—we'll get the body sewed up in it, so death won't
be before your eyes any longer.

(Wife throws out a pig's skin.)

WIFE: Oh no neighbor that won't do. I've got to wear that old red
coat of mine at my next wedding. Else I wouldn't have a thing to
wear. Look here. We can sew up my husband in this pig's skin.
The ol' hog got sick and died and the hide is spoiled for tanning
anyhow. I'd just have to throw it in the manure pile.

NEIGHBOR'S WIFE: Oh no! The hog's hide is much too short. It won't
even cover his body. The head will stick out on top. If you
don't want to use the red coat—you promised him when he was
alive—at least get out an old sheet.

WIFE: Never you mind, neighbor. We'll let the feet stick out! My dear
husband wouldn't care. Besides, I don't have an old sheet—the
worst I have is one that mother gave me in my hope chest. But
that's worth five cents!

NEIGHBOR'S WIFE: Oh come on! Bury him like an honest man. The
sheet is his going-away gift from this earth. Don't worry about
the cost. The good man was certainly worth it. Wait. Who's
knocking there?

(Wife opens the door. The Neighbor enters.)

NEIGHBOR: Tell me neighbor. Why did you lock the door? I was
afraid something had happened. I came to see what's wrong.

WIFE: Oh come in, dear neighbor. Oh my grief! My heartache! My husband's dead — I'm finished! I'd rather have all my livestock dead and gone!

NEIGHBOR: Oh neighbor, I'm so sorry to hear that. You loved him true. On my oath you did, if you'd give all your livestock to have him back. Tell me, what livestock do you have, anyway?

WIFE: Well, let's see. I've got here in the house a bird, a dog, a cat, two dozen mice, more or less, a dozen rats, bedbugs without number, fleas and lice. Yep, I'd give them all to have dear ol' Hans alive again.

NEIGHBOR: I can really see this love was enormous between you two. If you'd like to have him alive again, what if you made a vow — devoted three candles, perhaps a ball of flax, and an offering of silver. Maybe then he'd come back. It has been known to happen, you know, when a farmer came back to life.

WIFE: Oh dear neighbor, do be quiet! I'd rather save that expense. My husband's gone to heaven. It would be a shame and not right if I brought him back to earth with all this hardship and work. Isn't that right, neighbor?

NEIGHBOR: Well, let me go and just get a bier to lay him on and carry him to the church in a procession. Also let's not forget the candles and let's ring the bells.

WIFE: Oh neighbor do leave me alone! My Hans never liked such things. Take him over to the church on a manure wagon tonight after dark. Leave the priests and altar-boys at home. As for candles, we don't need them. He's dead and can't see anyway. Why ring the bells, he can't hear them. Why waste the money?

NEIGHBOR: Well, if we bury him today, there should at least be an offering tomorrow. A service with both young and old — so it will go well with his soul.

WIFE: Oh my husband hated to go to services and offerings. Why should we start after his death?

(She goes over to her husband and speaks above him.)

WIFE: Oh husband, what shall become of me? Shall I never see you alive again? Oh Hans, my dearly loved man, what shall I do now?

(Hans sits up and speaks.)

HANS: Ha! You just listen woman, and I'll tell you. Five eggs you fried in lard — and you sat there in the kitchen and swilled them down. Then you brought up a quart of wine and poured it all down your gullet! Go on! Go lay down and sober up! I've seen your great love that you brag about! You, you stupid nincompoop! You said you were going to bury me in your red coat—just now I couldn't even get a sheet out of you. You were going to sew me into a hog's hide. I've seen darn little love from you—neither in words or deeds. Ha! Your love reaches as far as the clothes and food I provide for you. If it weren't for that—you wouldn't look at me. Not even through a fence.

WIFE: Good grief, husband, I only did it to make fun of you. I knew all along you weren't dead. I knew you were just pretending. I knew you just wanted to see what I'd do. That's why I just played this trick on you. If you really died, I'd really act differently. Just ask your good neighbor how miserable I'd be.

NEIGHBOR: Neighbor, better forget this game. Your wife is full of cunning. You can't figure her out. She's got an excuse before she even looks down at the ground. My wife's the same. She uses just as much cunning. They're all alike. So let women be women. Let's go over together, have some wine and let's not let them get to us. Let's leave things as they are, and as they should be—so hopes Hans Sachs.

The Pregnant Farmer

(1559)

A Carnival Play

Kunz Turnipfumes, farmer   Heinz, farm-hand
Gretta, the farmer's wife   Isaac, Jewish doctor

(The farmer enters with his wife.)

KUNZ: Ohhh . . . Oh Gretta, my poor stomach . . . something is wrong. It can't be the wine. I haven't had a drink in nights. I didn't even try the new wine that sometimes gives me the runs or usually burns like fire down there. I dunno what it could be.

GRETTA: Now Kunz, I don't want to upset you but you know you were sittin' there in the sewing room last night eating one cold turnip right after another. My lord, you washed them all down with cold water. I tried, you know I did, I tried to get you to quit. I knew this would happen. Why, you tossed and turned in bed like an old cow. Back and forth the whole night.

KUNZ: I know, old girl, I know. But I was thinking about what Eberlein Groll was telling me last Saturday over at the bath house. He was tellin' me about this fellow Isaac, the Jew, who knows all sorts of stuff about medicine. I'll just send our farm-hand Heinz over there with this glass of my water.

GRETTA: Oh Kunz, good thinking. Just send him over with a couple of dollars. Well spent for a body's good. Yes, dear husband, that can only help you.

KUNZ: Heinz! Heinz! Come in here right now!

(Heinz enters.)

HEINZ: Yes sir. But what do you want, yelling me in here so?

KUNZ: Heinz, take this glass of my urine and ride like crazy to Sentelbach. Go to the inn and ask for the Jewish doctor, Isaac. When you see him, be polite and wish him a good day from me. Then show him my urine and have him tell me what's wrong. Ask him if he's got some medicine to help me. Tell him I'll be happy to pay; in fact, give him these two dollars for it.

(Heinz takes the glass of urine and money from his master.)

HEINZ: Yessir. I'll start right out. I'll ride lickety-split our old grey, half-blind donkey to Sentelbach. I'll go straight for the inn to find the Jew with his medicine. I'll be back in a hurry.

(Heinz shyly looks at the urine and exits.)

GRETTA: Come now, Kunz. Lie down a while and cover up snug as a bug. I'll go milk and feed the cow for you.

KUNZ: Oh woe is me. What a lousy time to get sick. I've got threshing to do. Darn it, this will set me back eighty bucks.

*(The farmer and farmer's wife exit. Isaac,
the Jew, enters talking to himself.)*

ISAAC: If my name isn't Isaac and if I don't come from Jewish stock, then I haven't made my living off prophesy and fortune-telling. Just let these farmers ask me where something was stolen, or where somebody buried such and such or hid it under the door mat, or carried off somebody's padlock. I give those farmers hocus-pocus blessings or tales of treasure or anything else I can think of to get a meal. But they started catching on to that. So now my new game is medicine instead of prophesies. I've never studied magic or medicine and they know I'm a fake in all the towns around here. But out here in the country these farmers will keep me fed. Ahh, how I love to go to these church fairs and show off my titles and fake degrees, and how I cured him and her and so-and-so. It's all baloney and bull. I don't know diddly about medicine. But, God, I can make a purge that will buzz and boom these farmers' guts. Ha! It's my cure-all. I cures one, I loses one. Me lose sleep? Hee-hee. Let's see now, I want to look out here and see if anybody is coming along the street with their pee glass in hand. I wonder if anybody is coming to my inn here? Anybody got some urine — nice red rotten — for me to yawn over for a couple of shekels?

(The Jew exits. Heinz, the farm-hand enters.)

HEINZ: Boy, talk about bad luck. How was I supposed to carry that stuff? Too bad. I had the pee in the glass riding the donkey over here to Sentelbach. But the dumb donkey can't see the tree roots he stumbles all over. Spilled the whole glass. Good thing he stopped to go. Gotta whole new glass. Gee, it's still warm too. I'll just take it to the smart Jew so he can see what's wrong with my master. He'll fix him fit as a fiddle. If not, and the boss dies, I'll take my chances with the missus. Even a blind man can fall on a horseshoe or lady luck. Guess I better go ask where to find the Jew and give him this pee.

(The farm-hand exits. The Jew enters speaking to himself.)

ISAAC: There is no business today at all. Nobody the whole morning. No urine to check. God, what shall I eat for lunch? I'll just diet or fast a bit, I can take it, or . . . the cat's got some stew meat there. Who cares? By night the farmers are all full and drunk. Who cares? I'll be thin forever. Damn. Isn't anybody sick today? What a sad song my heart mourns, by Jove!

(Heinz knocks.)

ISAAC: Who is knocking so clumsily there! Stop! Stop! I'm coming already.

(The Jew goes to the door. Heinz enters.)

HEINZ: Good day, sir. Can you tell me if you're called Sowsack the Jew? The fellow who knows medicine?

ISAAC: I'm not called Sowsack, dear man, my name is Isaac. What is your wish?

HEINZ: My boss, Kunz Turnipfumes, sent me over here from Grossenbach to see you on account of your medicine. You're supposed to look at his water and help him get rid of his sickness.

(The Jew looks at the urine.)

ISAAC: Hmm. Tell me where is it hurting him?

HEINZ: In bed, where I left him, I guess.

ISAAC: No, no. I meant which limb hurts him?

HEINZ: His stomach rumbles like stormy weather.

ISAAC: Could you tell me whether your boss has dropsy?

HEINZ: Ah! Well, he used to fall down the stairs at night sometimes.

(The Jew looks again at the urine.)

ISAAC: Is he coughing or vomiting?

HEINZ: Ha! Ha! He is coughing at both ends like big flames zooming out.

ISAAC: Young man, you are a coarse monkey. Tell me, is your master stopped or closed up?

HEINZ: No, no sir. Don't worry about that — the doors are wide open all the time.

ISAAC: I didn't mean that. Look just tell me if your master has wind and how he feels in his abdomen.

HEINZ: Oh, oh. I got you. Wind. Lord my master has wind to boot. Our house is out in the open. We've got too much wind most of the time.

ISAAC: I am not asking that. I just want to know if the patient farts.

HEINZ: Ha! Ha! Oh my master really does rip 'em. Just this mornin' he ripped one louder than an ox cloth tearin'. That half-dead hen flew out of her roost clear over to the threshing floor.

(The Jew studies the urine again.)

ISAAC: Oh, I see. That's good. Let me see if I understand. Has your master had the urge for a stool?

HEINZ: Oh sir. He's a farmer. What does he know about school? He weren't never near any school. He can only count hedges and do writin' with a pitchfork.

ISAAC: My God! Can't you understand a word? I'm asking simply if he has felt the desire to have a stool.

HEINZ: Oh. Oh. Oh yeah. That for sure. He has a stool, a bench, and several chairs. He feels like sittin' in all of 'em.

ISAAC: Good night! Just answer me please! Does your master . . . is he able to go comfortably?

HEINZ: Ah-hah. Now I get it. Of course, he's comfy. Sometimes he gets a lil' wobbly and weak-kneed. Heck, he just a lays there pantin' and puffin'. He ain't gonna out-run no more rabbits.

ISAAC: I didn't ask that! Just tell me clear and short. Can your master take a crap? Understand that Latin?

HEINZ: Ah, so that's what you been after? I dunno. But early this mornin' there was a cracklin' and a shoutin' and he laid a beaut of an egg. Over there behind the fence. Big as my felt hat too. Smelled like cabbage and was larded full with a hundred folds. Boy, the old sow rubbed and rolled it around 'til you couldn't find a snout full. Sir, do you need that too?

ISAAC: Now. Well now, we're getting there. That's a good sign. Let me look at this urine here. Let's see . . . that conforms with his illness. I'll have to prescribe the right medicine.

(The Jew looks very closely at the urine.)

ISAAC: Wonder of wonders! By my faith! The urine confirms it! Your master is pregnant with a filly! A colt! A foal! That's what's bellowing in his stomach. If I am to help him, he must take the strongest purge possible. He has to drive that filly right out of there. If he doesn't the filly will grow and grow and never get out alive. Hurry! He's got to get that filly out of there.

(Heinz takes the purge and gives Isaac two dollars.)

HEINZ: Here's your two dollars. I'm off as fast as I can.

(Heinz exits with the purge.)

ISAAC: Ha-ha! Now I've got enough for a glass of wine, some soup, and two rolls. That's going to have to be enough today, unless some more sick come over.

(The Jewish doctor exits. The farmer's wife leads the farmer on stage who is carrying a soup bowl and a tiny spoon.)

KUNZ: Oh Gretta, my stomach is killing me. Where's that Heinz? What's keeping him? He should have been back by now.

GRETTA: Now Kunz, you just sit down there on the bench a spell. Try to rest. Your poor tummy earned it. Here. Try to eat some of this soup.

(She pours the soup. The farmer eyes the small spoon and says angrily.)

KUNZ: How come you forgot my big tablespoon? What am I supposed to do with this thing?

GRETTA: Now, don't be angry, husband dear. It's just a little soup and for that you only need a little spoon.

(The farmer eats a spoonful or two and lets go of the spoon yelling.)

KUNZ: Oh me! Oh the pain! Double trouble. Who could see worse luck?

(The farmer throws the bowl on the floor. Coughs.)

GRETTA: Husband, what is it? Speak to me! Tell me!

KUNZ: The spoon! The spoon, I . . . swallowed it. Look here. The stem is . . . s-s-s-sticking out. Cough, cough, I'm, I'mm, I'm ch-o-k-ing.

(The wife hits him. Strokes his back.)

GRETTA: Oh dear! Dear, dear Kunz, I think you've swallowed it.

KUNZ: Oh now I'll be even sicker.

GRETTA: No wait. Here comes Heinz with your medicine.

(The farm-hand Heinz enters.)

HEINZ: Oh boss, I'm bringing bad news from the Jewish doctor. He saw your water and yelled that you were pregnant with a colt. Yep, a foal is growing right there in your gut.

(The farmer grabs his stomach.)

KUNZ: Oh no. Double disaster now rides against me. What! Am I gonna be the first horse-mother? A mare? Oh how am I s'posed to bring the thing out? What me suckle? I'm s'posed to be rough and tough. How can I flirt with the waitresses now? I'm the laughing stock of all men. Men and women alike will scorn me. Wife, you are to blame for this 'cuz you always want on top! That's how I got this foal. I'm gonna break your head open. My God! Oh my God! A colt! I would be better dead. My poor heart is breaking.

(Heinz approaches his master showing the purge.)

HEINZ: Hey boss, don't worry. Look here. The doctor gave me this purge for you to take. Just swallow this and your troubles will end. Why this very purge will drive that filly right out and you'll be Kunz Turnipfumes just like always. Here take it. It won't hurt you. Go on. Take it and down the hatch with that purge.

(Kunz takes and tastes the purge.)

KUNZ: Hey, what is this stuff? Wine or beer? God, it tastes like pure vinegar. Oh well. I'll just close my eyes and swallow the whole business.

*(The farmer drinks all of the purge and rubs
his stomach a moment and then shouts.)*

KUNZ: Pig shit! My God! It's like fire. It's rumbling now. Here, down here it's roaring and gnawing from below. Oh Lord, I've never felt worse in all my days. Watch out! The filly. It's coming out. Oh God, let me get outside where it's cool. Oh. Oh. Here Heinz steady me. Don't let me fall. Help me behind those hay bales.

(Heinz leads his master out while the wife speaks to herself.)

GRETTA: Who in all their born days ever heard tell of a farmer carrying a foal? Wish hubby would just give birth to it right now! Where oh where did he ever get pregnant? Hmm — wait a second. I wonder if it's cause he eats these oats. God knows he loves to eat the oats for the horses. I'll bet that's it. Yessir, he got pregnant from eating horse food. That's how the filly started to blossom right there in his stomach. Oh he's so impatient too. I just hope the foal is out by now. Oh my. I'd give three cents to have this mess over with. Oh dear, here comes the farm-hand Heinz right now.

(Heinz enters.)

HEINZ: Oh missus! Happy day! My master is alright. You should have heard the crack and crash as the spoon and the purge hit the barn door. He was breathin' in and out right there in front of the hedges. In and out. He was stretching and stretching and panting and panting. Then suddenly with a loud ka-shoom his back door opened up and that spoon and purge went a flyin'! With cracklin', rattlin', and splatterin' — a rabbit who must have been sleepin' behind the door — jumped up and ran off into the forest. When my master saw the rabbit, he thought it was his colt and he started to yell, "My child, come back! Stand still! Come drink from your mother!"

Just be sure, ma'am, when my master comes back in, you keep the secret. Don't tell him it was just a rabbit. He's restin' but he'll be strong soon. Wait here he comes now.

(The farmer enters.)

GRETTA: Dear husband, how was it? Did you give birth to your colt? Wonderful! Congratulations! I'm so proud of you.

KUNZ: Oh dear Gretta. Shouldn't I tell you in all my born days, by Jove, it was amazing! No filly has ever run like that. So fast and so swift . . . like an arrow. It went straight for the woods when it came out of my womb. Wife, I am telling you that when she grows up there won't be a horse her equal on earth. She ran so fast and quick I could sell her for eighty bucks . . . whew.

But never mind now. Go over there and get me a little soup and fix up my kinder-bed so I can lie down and rest for six weeks or so. I want you to cook real food for me, and you know I get wine three times a day! When the six weeks are up, I'll just take it easy for a while around the kitchen like the old and real young do. We'll go spend our carnival time with others. Let fun, frolic, and good times chase away sadness and misfortune. This is what Hans Sachs and his actors wish for you.

NOTES TO THE TEXTS

The Nose-Dance

1 This carnival play is one of Hans Sachs's oldest (1550). As such, it reflects the influence, style, and structure of the older fifteenth-century plays of the carnival genre. It is reminiscent of the sequential play; (*Rheihenspiel* or *Revuespiel*), which consisted of a series of characters delivering the same or similar types of monologues.
2 *Flegel* or flail is an appropriate name for one of the characters in this carnival play. The flail was a farm tool consisting of a free-swinging stick tied to the end of a long handle. The tool was used to thresh grain by hand.

The Stolen Bacon

1 *In Narribus phantastibus* is an unsuccessful attempt to render into Latin any meaningful sentence or thought appropriate to the action in the play. The result is mere gibberish. The use of macaronic Latin by Sachs was a favorite technique he used to ridicule and criticize an actual deficiency of some of the priests of his time.
2 *Gulden* or *Guilder* was a gold coin first issued in Florence in 1252. It was called a florin from the figure of a lily on the coin.

The Farmer with the Blur

1 *Bohnen* (beans) is a word-play on Bann (ban, excommunication). Heinz, in essence, is saying that he would rather face the threat of ban or some other form of religious sanction or punishment rather than forsake his Catholic religion for another; i.e., Protestant. This play, as well as several of the others, reflects the effects and conflicts of the Reformation in Germany.
2 Here Heinz says exactly what he means, but not what he has been tricked into believing. Hence, Gretta's next line, "More or less."

The Evil Woman

1 *Batzen*, obsolete German coin.
2 One of the few carnival plays that did not end with "and, so wishes" or "and so says Hans Sachs."

The Grand Inquisitor in the Soup

1 This carnival play represents perhaps the strongest censure by Hans Sachs of the abuses of some of the Catholic clergymen which eventually led to the schism of the Church in Germany and the subsequent Protestant Reformation.
2 This is one of the many examples of language distortion and word-play in the plays. Simon is fond of repeating what others say while mutilating one or two of the words at the same time.
3 Same as note number one of *The Farmer with the Blur*.

MEMBER OF SCABRINI GROUP

Québec, Canada
2006